O9-CFT-576

I PLEDGE

that over the coming year I will meet the public standard described in the book and give at least the amount specified, in accordance with my income level, to an organization helping people living in extreme poverty.

_____   _____

_____   _____

_____   _____

_____   _____

_____   _____

_____   _____

_____   _____

_____   _____

_____   _____

_____   _____

_____   _____

_____   _____

_____   _____

Keep this book working for the poor. Pass it on to someone else.

When this page is full, please mail a copy to:

Peter Singer
University Center for Human Values
Princeton University
5 Ivy Lane, Princeton, NJ 08544 –1013
USA

Or fax it:
+1 609 258 1285

Or scan and e-mail it:
info@thelifeyoucansave.com

That way, we can add the signatures to the total number of pledgers.
For more information, please visit www.thelifeyoucansave.com. Thanks.

Praise for
The Life You Can Save

"Mr. Singer is far from the world's only serious thinker on poverty, but with *The Life You Can Save* he becomes, instantly, its most readable and lapel-grabbing one." —*The New York Times*

"Mr. Singer is a compelling moral voice seeking far more compassion for those who have the least." —*The Wall Street Journal*

"Singer's arguments are powerful and well thought out, and he offers a wealth of examples to demonstrate his argument that the wealthiest people in the developed world should give up enough of their wealth to reduce extreme poverty in the world." —*Journal Inquirer*

"Powerful and clarifying . . . Singer sets up a demanding ethical compass for human behavior." —*Sunday Star Ledger*

"This short and surprisingly compelling book sets out to answer two difficult questions: why people in affluent countries should donate money to fight global poverty and how much each should give. . . . Singer doesn't ask readers to choose between asceticism and self-indulgence; his solution can be found in the middle, and it is reasonable and rewarding for all." —*Publishers Weekly* (starred review)

"If you think you can't afford to give money to the needy, I urge you to read this book. If you think you're already giving enough, and to the right places, still I urge you to read this book. In *The Life You Can Save,* Peter Singer makes a strong case—logical and factual, but also emotional—for why each of us should be doing more for the world's impoverished. This book will challenge you to be a better person."
—HOLDEN KARNOFSKY, co-founder, GiveWell

"Peter Singer challenges each of us to ask: Am I willing to make poverty history? Skillfully weaving together parable, philosophy, and hard statistics, he tackles the most familiar moral, ethical, and ideological obstacles to building a global culture of philanthropy, and sets the bar for how we as citizens might do our part to empower the world's poor."
—RAYMOND C. OFFENHEISER, president, Oxfam America

BY PETER SINGER

The Grandest Challenge

The Life You Can Save

Democracy and Disobedience

Animal Liberation

Practical Ethics

Marx

Animal Factories (with James Mason)

The Expanding Circle

Hegel

The Reproduction Revolution (with Dean Wells)

Should the Baby Live? (with Helga Kuhse)

How Are We to Live?

Rethinking Life and Death

Ethics into Action

A Darwinian Left

Writings on an Ethical Life

Unsanctifying Human Life (edited by Helga Kuhse)

One World

Pushing Time Away

The President of Good and Evil

How Ethical Is Australia? (with Tom Gregg)

The Ethics of What We Eat (with Jim Mason)

THE LIFE
YOU CAN SAVE

THE LIFE
YOU CAN SAVE

How to Do Your Part
to End World Poverty

PETER SINGER

RANDOM HOUSE TRADE PAPERBACKS  NEW YORK

2010 Random House Trade Paperback Edition

Copyright © 2009 by Peter Singer
Afterword copyright © 2010 by Peter Singer

Published in the United States by
Random House Trade Paperbacks,
an imprint of The Random House Publishing Group,
a division of Random House, Inc., New York.

RANDOM HOUSE TRADE PAPERBACKS and colophon
are trademarks of Random House, Inc.

Originally published in hardcover in the United States by
Random House, an imprint of The Random House Publishing
Group, a division of Random House, Inc., in 2009.

Library of Congress Cataloging-in-Publication Data

Singer, Peter
    The life you can save : how to do your part to end world
    poverty / Peter Singer
        p. cm.
    Includes index.
    ISBN 978-0-8129-8156-8
    1. Charity. 2. Humanitarianism. 3. Economic assistance.
    4. Poverty. I. Title.
    HV48.S56 2009
    362.5—dc22   2008036279

Printed in the United States of America

www.atrandom.com

9 8 7

Book design by Liz Cosgrove

To Renata, without whom . . .

Contents

Preface

When he saw the man fall onto the subway tracks, Wesley Autry didn't hesitate. With the lights of the oncoming train visible, Autry, a construction worker, jumped down to the tracks and pushed the man down into a drainage trench between the rails, covering him with his own body. The train passed over them, leaving a trail of grease on Autry's cap. Autry, later invited to the State of the Union Address and praised by the president for his bravery, downplayed his actions: "I don't feel like I did something spectacular. I just saw someone who needed help. I did what I felt was right."[1]

What if I told you that you, too, can save a life, even many lives? Do you have a bottle of water or a can of soda on the table beside you as you read this book? If you are paying for something to drink when safe drinking water comes out of the tap, you have money to spend on things you don't really need. Around the world, a billion people struggle to live each day on less than you paid for that drink. Because they can't afford even the most basic health care for their families, their children may die from simple, easily treatable diseases like diarrhea. You can help them, and you don't have to risk getting hit by an oncoming train to do it.

I have been thinking and writing for more than thirty years about how we should respond to hunger and poverty. I have presented this book's argument to thousands of students in my university classes and in lectures around the world, and to countless others in newspapers, magazines, and television programs. As a result, I've been forced to respond to a wide range

of thoughtful challenges. This book represents my effort to dis-
till what I've learned about why we give, or don't give, and what
we should do about it.

We live in a unique moment. The proportion of people unable to meet their basic physical needs is smaller today than it
has been at any time in recent history, and perhaps at any time
since humans first came into existence. At the same time, when
we take a long-term perspective that sees beyond the fluctua-
tions of the economic cycle, the proportion of people with far
more than they need is also unprecedented. Most important,
rich and poor are now linked in ways they never were before.
Moving images, in real time, of people on the edge of survival
are beamed into our living rooms. Not only do we know a lot
about the desperately poor, but we also have much more to
offer them in terms of better health care, improved seeds and
agricultural techniques, and new technologies for generating
electricity. More amazing, through instant communications
and open access to a wealth of information that surpasses the
greatest libraries of the pre-Internet age, we can enable them to
join the worldwide community—if only we can help them get
far enough out of poverty to seize the opportunity.

Economist Jeffrey Sachs has argued convincingly that extreme poverty can be virtually eliminated by the middle of
this century. We are already making progress. In 1960, according to UNICEF, the United Nations International Children's Emergency Fund, 20 million children died before their
fifth birthday because of poverty. In 2007, UNICEF announced that, for the first time since record keeping began, the
number of deaths of young children has fallen below 10 million a year.[2] Public health campaigns against smallpox, measles,
and malaria have contributed to the drop in child mortality, as
has economic progress in several countries. The drop is even
more impressive because the world's population has more than
doubled since 1960. Yet we can't become complacent: 9.7 mil-

lion children under five still die annually; this is an immense tragedy, not to mention a moral stain on a world as rich as this one. And the combination of economic uncertainty and volatile food prices that marked 2008 could still reverse the downward trend in poverty-related deaths.

We can liken our situation to an attempt to reach the summit of an immense mountain. For all the eons of human existence, we have been climbing up through dense cloud. We haven't known how far we have to go, nor whether it is even possible to get to the top. Now at last we have emerged from the mist and can see a route up the remaining steep slopes and onto the summit ridge. The peak still lies some distance ahead. There are sections of the route that will challenge our abilities to the utmost, but we can see that the ascent is feasible.

We can, each of us, do our part in this epoch-making climb. In recent years there's been a good deal of coverage of some among the very rich who have taken on this challenge in a bold and public way. Warren Buffett has pledged to give $31 billion, and Bill and Melinda Gates have given $29 billion and are planning to give more.[3] Immense as these sums are, we will see by the end of this book that they are only a small fraction of what people in rich nations could easily give, without a significant reduction in their standard of living. We won't reach our goal unless many more contribute to the effort.

That's why this is the right time to ask yourself: What ought I be doing to help?

I write this book with two linked but significantly different goals. The first is to challenge you to think about our obligations to those trapped in extreme poverty. The part of the book that lays out this challenge will deliberately present a very demanding—some might even say impossible—standard of ethical behavior. I'll suggest that it may not be possible to consider ourselves to be living a morally good life unless we give a great deal more than most of us would think it realistic to expect human beings to give. This may sound absurd, and yet the argument for it is remarkably simple. It goes back to that bottle of water, to the money we spend on things that aren't *really* necessary. If it is so easy to help people in real need through no fault of their own, and yet we fail to do so, aren't we doing something wrong? At a minimum, I hope this book will persuade you that there is something deeply askew with our widely accepted views about what it is to live a good life.

The second goal of this book is to convince you to choose to give more of your income to help the poor. You'll be happy to know that I fully realize the need to step back from the demanding standards of a philosophical argument to ask what will really make a difference in the way we act. I'll consider the reasons, some relatively convincing, others less so, that we offer for not giving, as well as the psychological factors that get in our way. I'll acknowledge the bounds of human nature and yet provide examples of people who seem to have found a way to push those bounds further than most. And I will close with a reasonable standard that, for 95 percent of Americans, can be met by giving no more than 5 percent of their income.

I should say up front that I believe you should be giving more than 5 percent, and that I hope you'll ultimately move in that direction. But that's not easy to hear and not easy to do. I recognize that most people aren't likely to be moved merely by philosophical argument to make drastic changes in the way they live, and, further, that one cannot make such drastic changes overnight. The ultimate purpose of this book is to reduce extreme poverty, not to make you feel guilty. So I'm going to advocate a standard that I'm confident will do a lot of good. That means suggesting a level that will get you started, and put you on a path toward challenging yourself and working toward doing more.

For reasons that I'll explore in this book, many of us find it difficult to consider giving money to people we've never met, living in distant countries we've never visited. This obviously doesn't get any easier during periods of economic uncertainty, when many people are justifiably anxious about their own economic prospects. While I don't seek to diminish in any way the challenges that attend tough economic times, we should remember that even in the worst of times, our lives remain infinitely better than those of people living in extreme poverty. I'm hoping that you will look at the larger picture and think about what it takes to live ethically in a world in which 18 million people are dying unnecessarily each year. That's a higher annual death rate than in World War II. In the past twenty years alone, it adds up to more deaths than were caused by all the civil and international wars and government repression of the entire twentieth century, the century of Hitler and Stalin. How much would we give to prevent those horrors? Yet how little are we doing to prevent today's even larger toll, and all the misery that it involves? I believe that if you read this book to the end, and look honestly and carefully at our situation, assessing both the facts and the ethical arguments, you will agree that we must act.

PETER SINGER

THE ARGUMENT

1. Saving a Child

On your way to work, you pass a small pond. On hot days, children sometimes play in the pond, which is only about knee-deep. The weather's cool today, though, and the hour is early, so you are surprised to see a child splashing about in the pond. As you get closer, you see that it is a very young child, just a toddler, who is flailing about, unable to stay upright or walk out of the pond. You look for the parents or babysitter, but there is no one else around. The child is unable to keep his head above the water for more than a few seconds at a time. If you don't wade in and pull him out, he seems likely to drown. Wading in is easy and safe, but you will ruin the new shoes you bought only a few days ago, and get your suit wet and muddy. By the time you hand the child over to someone responsible for him, and change your clothes, you'll be late for work. What should you do?

I teach a course called Practical Ethics. When we start talking about global poverty, I ask my students what they think you should do in this situation. Predictably, they respond that you should save the child. "What about your shoes? And being late for work?" I ask them. They brush that aside. How could anyone consider a pair of shoes, or missing an hour or two at work, a good reason for not saving a child's life?

In 2007, something resembling this hypothetical situation actually occurred near Manchester, England. Jordon Lyon, a ten-year-old boy, leaped into a pond after his stepsister Bethany slipped in. He struggled to support her but went under himself. Anglers managed to pull Bethany out, but by then Jordon could no longer be seen. They raised the alarm, and two police community support officers soon arrived; they refused to enter the pond to find Jordon. He was later pulled out, but attempts at resuscitation failed. At the inquest on Jordon's death, the officers' inaction was defended on the grounds that they had not been trained to deal with such situations. The mother responded: "If you're walking down the street and you see a child drowning you automatically go in that water . . . You don't have to be trained to jump in after a drowning child."[1]

I think it's safe to assume that most people would agree with the mother's statement. But consider that, according to UNICEF, nearly 10 million children under five years old die each year from causes related to poverty. Here is just one case, described by a man in Ghana to a researcher from the World Bank:

> Take the death of this small boy this morning, for example. The boy died of measles. We all know he could have been cured at the hospital. But the parents had no money and so the boy died a slow and painful death, not of measles but out of poverty.[2]

Think about something like that happening 27,000 times every day. Some children die because they don't have enough to eat. More die, like that small boy in Ghana, from measles, malaria, and diarrhea, conditions that either don't exist in developed nations, or, if they do, are almost never fatal. The children are vulnerable to these diseases because they have no safe drinking water, or no sanitation, and because when they do fall ill, their parents can't afford any medical treatment. UNICEF, Oxfam, and many other organizations are working to reduce poverty and provide clean water and basic health care, and these efforts are reducing the toll. If the relief organizations had more money, they could do more, and more lives would be saved.

Now think about your own situation. By donating a relatively small amount of money, you could save a child's life. Maybe it takes more than the amount needed to buy a pair of shoes—but we all spend money on things we don't really need, whether on drinks, meals out, clothing, movies, concerts, vacations, new cars, or house renovation. Is it possible that by choosing to spend your money on such things rather than contributing to an aid agency, you are leaving a child to die, a child you could have saved?

Poverty Today

A few years ago, the World Bank asked researchers to listen to what the poor are saying. They were able to document the experiences of 60,000 women and men in seventy-three countries. Over and over, in different languages and on different continents, poor people said that poverty meant these things:

- You are short of food for all or part of the year, often eating only one meal per day, sometimes having to choose between stilling your child's hunger or your own, and sometimes being able to do neither.

- You can't save money. If a family member falls ill and you need money to see a doctor, or if the crop fails and you have nothing to eat, you have to borrow from a local moneylender and he will charge you so much interest as the debt continues to mount and you may never be free of it.

- You can't afford to send your children to school, or if they do start school, you have to take them out again if the harvest is poor.

- You live in an unstable house, made with mud or thatch that you need to rebuild every two or three years, or after severe weather.

- You have no nearby source of safe drinking water. You have to carry your water a long way, and even then, it can make you ill unless you boil it.

But extreme poverty is not only a condition of unsatisfied material needs. It is often accompanied by a degrading state of powerlessness. Even in countries that are democracies and are relatively well governed, respondents to the World Bank survey described a range of situations in which they had to accept humiliation without protest. If someone takes what little you have, and you complain to the police, they may not listen to you. Nor will the law necessarily protect you from rape or sexual harassment. You have a pervading sense of shame and failure because you cannot provide for your children. Your poverty traps you, and you lose hope of ever escaping from a life of hard work for which, at the end, you will have nothing to show beyond bare survival.[3]

The World Bank defines extreme poverty as not having enough income to meet the most basic human needs for adequate food, water, shelter, clothing, sanitation, health care, and education. Many people are familiar with the statistic that

1 billion people are living on less than one dollar per day. That was the World Bank's poverty line until 2008, when better data on international price comparisons enabled it to make a more accurate calculation of the amount people need to meet their basic needs. On the basis of this calculation, the World Bank set the poverty line at $1.25 per day. The number of people whose income puts them under this line is not 1 billion but 1.4 billion. That there are more people living in extreme poverty than we thought is, of course, bad news, but the news is not all bad. On the same basis, in 1981 there were 1.9 billion people living in extreme poverty. That was about four in every ten people on the planet, whereas now fewer than one in four are extremely poor.

South Asia is still the region with the largest number of people living in extreme poverty, a total of 600 million, including 455 million in India. Economic growth has, however, reduced the proportion of South Asians living in extreme poverty from 60 percent in 1981 to 42 percent in 2005. There are another 380 million extremely poor people in sub-Saharan Africa, where half the population is extremely poor—and that is the same percentage as in 1981. The most dramatic reduction in poverty has been in East Asia, although there are still more than 200 million extremely poor Chinese, and smaller numbers elsewhere in the region. The remaining extremely poor people are distributed around the world, in Latin America and the Caribbean, the Pacific, the Middle East, North Africa, Eastern Europe, and Central Asia.[4]

In response to the "$1.25 a day" figure, the thought may cross your mind that in many developing countries, it is possible to live much more cheaply than in the industrialized nations. Perhaps you have even done it yourself, backpacking around the world, living on less than you would have believed possible. So you may imagine that this level of poverty is less extreme than it would be if you had to live on that amount of money in the United States, or any industrialized nation. If such thoughts did occur to you, you should banish them now, because the World Bank has already made the adjustment in purchasing power: Its figures refer to the number of people existing on a daily total consumption of goods and services—whether earned or home-grown—comparable to the amount of goods and services that can be bought in the United States for $1.25.

In wealthy societies, most poverty is relative. People feel poor because many of the good things they see advertised on television are beyond their budget—but they do have a television. In the United States, 97 percent of those classified by the Census Bureau as poor own a color TV. Three quarters of them own a car. Three quarters of them have air-conditioning. Three quarters of them have a VCR or DVD player. All have access to health care.[5] I am not quoting these figures in order to deny that the poor in the United States face genuine difficulties. Nevertheless, for most, these difficulties are of a different order than those of the world's poorest people. The 1.4 billion people living in extreme poverty are poor by an absolute standard tied to the most basic human needs. They are likely to be hungry for at least part of each year. Even if they can get enough food to fill their stomachs, they will probably be malnourished because their diet lacks essential nutrients. In children, malnutrition stunts growth and can cause permanent brain damage. The poor may not be able to afford to send their children to school. Even minimal health care services are usually beyond their means.

This kind of poverty kills. Life expectancy in rich nations averages seventy-eight years; in the poorest nations, those officially classified as "least developed," it is below fifty.[6] In rich countries, fewer than one in a hundred children die before the age of five; in the poorest countries, one in five does. And to the UNICEF figure of nearly 10 million young children dying every year from avoidable, poverty-related causes, we must add at least another 8 million older children and adults.[7]

Affluence Today

Roughly matching the 1.4 billion people living in extreme poverty, there are about a billion living at a level of affluence never previously known except in the courts of kings and nobles. As king of France, Louis XIV, the "Sun King," could afford to build the most magnificent palace Europe had ever seen, but he could not keep it cool in summer as effectively as most middle-class people in industrialized nations can keep their homes cool today. His gardeners, for all their skill, were unable to produce the variety of fresh fruits and vegetables that we can buy all year-round. If he developed a toothache or fell ill, the best his dentists and doctors could do for him would make us shudder.

But we're not just better off than a French king who lived centuries ago. We are also much better off than our own great-grandparents. For a start, we can expect to live about thirty years longer. A century ago, one child in ten died in infancy. Now, in most rich nations, that figure is less than one in two hundred.[8] Another telling indicator of how wealthy we are today is the modest number of hours we must work in order to meet our basic dietary needs. Today Americans spend, on average, only 6 percent of their income on buying food. If they work a forty-hour week, it takes them barely two hours to earn enough to feed themselves for the week. That leaves far more to spend on consumer goods, entertainment, and vacations.

And then we have the superrich, people who spend their money on palatial homes, ridiculously large and luxurious boats, and private planes. Before the 2008 stock market crash trimmed the numbers, there were more than 1,100 billionaires in the world, with a combined net worth of $4.4 trillion.[9] To cater to such people, Lufthansa Technik unveiled its plans for a private configuration of Boeing's new 787 Dreamliner. In commercial service, this plane will seat up to 330 passengers. The private version will carry 35, at a price of $150 million. Cost aside, there's nothing like owning a really big airplane carrying a small number of people to maximize your personal contribution to global warming. Apparently, there are already several billionaires who fly around in private commercial-sized airliners, from 747s down. Larry Page and Sergey Brin, the Google cofounders, reportedly bought a Boeing 767 and spent millions fitting it out for their private use.[10] But for conspicuous waste of money and resources it is hard to beat Anousheh Ansari, an Iranian-American telecommunications entrepreneur who paid a reported $20 million for eleven days in space. Comedian Lewis Black said on Jon Stewart's *The Daily Show* that Ansari did it because it was "the only way she could achieve her life's goal of flying over every single starving person on earth and yelling 'Hey, look what I'm spending my money on!' "

While I was working on this book, a special advertising supplement fell out of my Sunday edition of *The New York Times*: a sixty-eight-page glossy magazine filled with advertising for watches by Rolex, Patek Philippe, Breitling, and other luxury brands. The ads didn't carry price tags, but a puff piece about the revival of the mechanical watch gave guidance about the lower end of the range. After admitting that inexpensive quartz watches are extremely accurate and functional, the article opined that there is "something engaging about a mechanical movement." Right, but how much will it cost you to have this engaging something on your wrist? "You might think that getting into mechanical watches is an expensive proposition, but there are plenty of choices in the $500–$5000 range." Admittedly, "these opening-price-point models are pretty simple:

basic movement, basic time display, simple decoration and so on." From which we can gather that most of the watches advertised are priced upward of $5,000, or more than one hundred times what anyone needs to pay for a reliable, accurate quartz watch. That there is a market for such products—and one worth advertising at such expense to the wide readership of *The New York Times*—is another indication of the affluence of our society.[11]

If you're shaking your head at the excesses of the superrich, though, don't shake too hard. Think again about some of the ways Americans with average incomes spend their money. In most places in the United States, you can get your recommended eight glasses of water a day out of the tap for less than a penny, while a bottle of water will set you back $1.50 or more.[12] And in spite of the environmental concerns raised by the waste of energy that goes into producing and transporting it, Americans are still buying bottled water, to the tune of more than 31 billion liters in 2006.[13] Think, too, of the way many of us get our caffeine fix: You can make coffee at home for pennies rather than spending three dollars or more on a latte. Or have you ever casually said yes to a waiter's prompt to order a second soda or glass of wine that you didn't even finish? When Dr. Timothy Jones, an archaeologist, led a U.S. goverment–funded study of food waste, he found that 14 percent of household garbage is perfectly good food that was in its original packaging and not out of date. More than half of this food was dry-packaged or canned goods that keep for a long time. According to Jones, $100 billion of food is wasted in the United States every year.[14] Fashion designer Deborah Lindquist claims that the average woman owns more than $600 worth of clothing that she has not worn in the last year.[15] Whatever the actual figure may be, it is fair to say that almost all of us, men and women alike, buy things we don't need, some of which we never even use.

Most of us are absolutely certain that we wouldn't hesitate to save a drowning child, and that we would do it at considerable cost to ourselves. Yet while thousands of children die each day, we spend money on things we take for granted and would hardly notice if they were not there. Is that wrong? If so, how far does our obligation to the poor go?

2. Is It Wrong Not to Help?

Bob is close to retirement. He has invested most of his savings in a very rare and valuable old car, a Bugatti, which he has not been able to insure. The Bugatti is his pride and joy. Not only does Bob get pleasure from driving and caring for his car, he also knows that its rising market value means that he will be able to sell it and live comfortably after retirement. One day when Bob is out for a drive, he parks the Bugatti near the end of a railway siding and goes for a walk up the track. As he does so, he sees that a runaway train, with no one aboard, is rolling down the railway track. Looking farther down the track, he sees the small figure of a child who appears to be absorbed in playing on the tracks. Oblivious to the runaway train, the child is in great danger. Bob can't stop the train, and the child is too far away to hear his warning shout, but Bob can throw a switch that will divert the train down the siding where his Bugatti is parked. If he does so, nobody will be killed, but the train will crash through the decaying barrier at the end of the siding and destroy his Bugatti. Thinking of his joy in owning the car and the financial security it represents, Bob decides not to throw the switch.

The car or the child?

Philosopher Peter Unger developed this variation on the story of the drowning child to challenge us to think further about how much we believe we should sacrifice in order to save the life of a child. Unger's story adds a factor often crucial to our thinking about real-world poverty: uncertainty about the outcome of our sacrifice. Bob cannot be certain that the child will die if he does nothing and saves his car. Perhaps at the last moment the child will hear the train and leap to safety. In the same way, most of us can summon doubts about whether the money we give to a charity is really helping the people it's intended to help.

In my experience, people almost always respond that Bob acted badly when he did not throw the switch and destroy his most cherished and valuable possession, thereby sacrificing his hope of a financially secure retirement. We can't take a serious risk with a child's life, they say, merely to save a car, no matter how rare and valuable the car may be. By implication, we should also believe that with the simple act of saving money for retirement, we are acting as badly as Bob. For in saving money for retirement, we are effectively refusing to use that money to help save lives. This is a difficult implication to confront. How can it be wrong to save for a comfortable retirement? There is, at the very least, something puzzling here.

Another example devised by Unger tests the level of sacrifice we think people should make to alleviate suffering in cases when a life is not at stake:

> You are driving your vintage sedan down a country lane when you are stopped by a hiker who has seriously injured

his leg. He asks you to take him to the nearest hospital. If you refuse, there is a good chance that he will lose his leg. On the other hand, if you agree to take him to hospital, he is likely to bleed onto the seats, which you have recently, and expensively, restored in soft white leather.

Again, most people respond that you should drive the hiker to the hospital. This suggests that when prompted to think in concrete terms, about real individuals, most of us consider it obligatory to lessen the serious suffering of innocent others, even at some cost (even a high cost) to ourselves.[1]

The Basic Argument

The above examples reveal our intuitive belief that we ought to help others in need, at least when we can see them and when we are the only person in a position to save them. But our moral intuitions are not always reliable, as we can see from variations in what people in different times and places find intuitively acceptable or objectionable. The case for helping those in extreme poverty will be stronger if it does not rest solely on our intuitions. Here is a logical argument from plausible premises to the same conclusion.

> First premise: Suffering and death from lack of food, shelter, and medical care are bad.
> Second premise: If it is in your power to prevent something bad from happening, without sacrificing anything nearly as important, it is wrong not to do so.
> Third premise: By donating to aid agencies, you can prevent suffering and death from lack of food, shelter, and medical care, without sacrificing anything nearly as important.

Conclusion: Therefore, if you do not donate to aid agencies, you are doing something wrong.

The drowning-child story is an application of this argument for aid, since ruining your shoes and being late for work aren't nearly as important as the life of a child. Similarly, reupholstering a car is not nearly as big a deal as losing a leg. Even in the case of Bob and the Bugatti, it would be a big stretch to suggest that the loss of the Bugatti would come close to rivaling the significance of the death of an innocent person.

Ask yourself if you can deny the premises of the argument. How could suffering and death from lack of food, shelter, and medical care not be really, really bad? Think of that small boy in Ghana who died of measles. How you would feel if you were his mother or father, watching helplessly as your son suffers and grows weaker? You know that children often die from this condition. You also know that it would be curable, if only you could afford to take your child to a hospital. In those circumstances you would give up almost anything for some way of ensuring your child's survival.

Putting yourself in the place of others, like the parents of that boy, or the child himself, is what thinking ethically is all about. It is encapsulated in the Golden Rule, "Do unto others as you would have them do unto you." Though the Golden Rule is best known to most westerners from the words of Jesus as reported by Matthew and Luke, it is remarkably universal, being found in Buddhism, Confucianism, Hinduism, Islam, and Jainism, and in Judaism, where it is found in Leviticus, and later emphasized by the sage Hillel.[2] The Golden Rule requires us to accept that the desires of others ought to count as if they were our own. If the desires of the parents of the dying child were our own, we would have no doubt that their suffering and the death of their child are about as bad as anything can be. So if we think ethically, then those desires must count as if they were our own, and we cannot deny that the suffering and death are bad.

The second premise is also very difficult to reject, because it leaves us some wiggle room when it comes to situations in which, to prevent something bad, we would have to risk something *nearly* as important as the bad thing we are preventing. Consider, for example, a situation in which you can only prevent the deaths of other children by neglecting your own children. This standard does not require you to prevent the deaths of the other children.

"Nearly as important" is a vague term. That's deliberate, because I'm confident that you can do without plenty of things that are clearly and inarguably not as valuable as saving a child's life. I don't know what *you* might think is as important, or nearly as important, as saving a life. By leaving it up to you to decide what those things are, I can avoid the need to find out. I'll trust you to be honest with yourself about it.

Analogies and stories can be pushed too far. Rescuing a child drowning in front of you, and throwing a switch on a railroad track to save the life of a child you can see in the distance, where you are the only one who can save the child, are both different from giving aid to people who are far away. The argument I have just presented complements the drowning-child case, because instead of pulling at your heartstrings by focusing on a single child in need, it appeals to your reason and seeks your assent to an abstract but compelling moral principle. That means that to reject it, you need to find a flaw in the reasoning.

You might now be thinking to yourself that the basic argument—that we should donate to aid agencies when by doing so we can prevent suffering and death without giving up anything nearly as important—isn't all that controversial. Yet if we were to take it seriously, our lives would be changed dramatically. For while the cost of saving one child's life by a donation to an aid organization may not be great, after you have donated that sum, there remain more children in need of saving, each one of whom can be saved at a relatively small additional cost. Suppose you have just sent $200 to an agency that can, for that amount, save the life of a child in a developing country who would otherwise have died. You've done something really good, and all it has cost you is the price of some new clothes you didn't really need anyway. Congratulations! But don't celebrate your good deed by opening a bottle of champagne, or even going to a movie. The cost of that bottle or movie, added to what you could save by cutting down on a few other extravagances, would save the life of another child. After you forgo those items, and give another $200, though, is everything else you are spending on as important, or nearly as important, as the life of a child? Not likely! So you must keep cutting back on unnecessary spending, and donating what you save, until you have reduced yourself to the point where if you give any more, you will be sacrificing something nearly as important as a child's life—like giving so much that you can no longer afford to give your children an adequate education.

We tend to assume that if people do not harm others, keep their promises, do not lie or cheat, support their children and their elderly parents, and perhaps contribute a little to needier members of their local community, they've done well. If we have money left over after meeting our needs and those of our dependents, we may spend it as we please. Giving to strangers, especially those beyond one's community, may be good, but we don't think of it as something we *have* to do. But if the basic argument presented above is right, then what many of us consider acceptable behavior must be viewed in a new, more ominous light. When we spend our surplus on concerts or fashionable shoes, on fine dining and good wines, or on holidays in faraway lands, we are doing something wrong.

Suddenly the three premises laid out above are much harder

to swallow. You may now be questioning whether a moral argument that has such radically demanding implications can possibly be sound. And so it's worth stepping back a moment to look at how this argument fits into some of our most respected ethical traditions.

Traditional Views on Helping the Poor

In the Christian tradition, helping the poor is a requirement for salvation. Jesus told the rich man: "If you want to be perfect, go, sell your possessions and give to the poor." To make sure his message wasn't missed, he went on to say that it is easier for a camel to go through the eye of a needle than for a rich man to enter the kingdom of God.[3] He praised the Good Samaritan who went out of his way to help a stranger.[4] He urged those who give feasts to invite the poor, the maimed, the lame, and the blind.[5] When he spoke of the last judgment, he said that God will save those who have fed the hungry, given drink to the thirsty, and clothed the naked. It is how we act toward "the least of these brothers of mine" that will determine, Jesus says, whether we inherit the kingdom of God or go into the eternal fire.[6] He places far more emphasis on charity for the poor than on anything else.

Not surprisingly, early and medieval Christians took these teachings very seriously. Paul, in his second letter to the Corinthians, proposed that those with a surplus should share with the needy: "Your surplus at the present time should supply their needs, so that their surplus may also supply your needs, that there may be equality."[7] The members of the early Christian community in Jerusalem, according to the account given in the Acts of the Apostles, sold all their possessions and divided them according to need.[8] The Franciscans, the order of monks founded by Francis of Assisi, took a vow of poverty and renounced all private property. Thomas Aquinas, the great medieval scholar whose ideas became the semi-official philosophy of the Roman Catholic church, wrote that whatever we have in "superabundance"—that is, above and beyond what will reasonably satisfy our own needs and those of our family, for the present and the foreseeable future—"is owed, of natural right, to the poor for their sustenance." In support of this view, he quoted Ambrose, one of the four original "Great Doctors" or teachers of the Church. He also cited the Decretum Gratiani, a twelfth-century compilation of canon law that contains the powerful statement, "The bread which you withhold belongs to the hungry: the clothing you shut away, to the naked: and the money you bury in the earth is the redemption and freedom of the penniless."

Note that "owed" and "belongs." For these Christians, sharing our surplus wealth with the poor is not a matter of charity, but of our duty and their rights. Aquinas even went so far as to say: "It is not theft, properly speaking, to take secretly and use another's property in a case of extreme need: because that which he takes for the support of his life becomes his own property by reason of that need."[9] This isn't just a Roman Catholic view. John Locke, the favorite philosopher of America's founding fathers, wrote that "charity gives every man a title to so much out of another's plenty, as will keep him from extreme want, where he has no means to subsist otherwise."[10]

Today, some Christians are seeking a renewed focus on the message of the gospels. Jim Wallis, founder and editor of the Christian magazine *Sojourners,* likes to point out that the Bible contains more than three thousand references to alleviating poverty—enough reason, he thinks, for making this a central moral issue for Christians.[11] Rick Warren, author of *The Purpose Driven Life* and pastor of the Saddleback Church, visited South Africa in 2003 and came across a tiny church operating from a dilapidated tent and sheltering twenty-five children orphaned by AIDS. This was, Warren says, "like a knife in the heart: I realized they were doing more for the poor than my entire megachurch." Since then, with his encouragement, more than 7,500 Saddleback Church members have paid their own way to developing countries to do volunteer work fighting poverty and disease. Once they have seen the situation for themselves, many want to keep helping. Warren himself now says, "I couldn't care less about politics, the culture wars. My only interest is to get people to care about Darfurs and Rwandas."[12]

Helping the poor is also strongly emphasized in Judaism, the source of many of those three thousand biblical references to helping the poor. The Hebrew word for "charity," *tzedakah,* simply means "justice" and, as this suggests, for Jews, giving to the poor is no optional extra but an essential part of living a just life. In the Talmud (a record of discussions of Jewish law and ethics by ancient rabbis) it is said that charity is equal in importance to all the other commandments combined, and that Jews should give at least 10 percent of their income as *tzedakah.*[13]

Islam, too, requires its adherents to help those in need. Each year, Muslims above a minimum level of wealth must give *zakat* in proportion to their assets (not income). For gold and silver—which today are understood to include cash and other liquid assets—the requirement is to give 2.5 percent every year. In addition, one may give *sadaqa,* which may include both money and labor—for example, digging a well so that travelers will have water, or helping build a mosque. Unlike *zakat, sadaqa* is optional.

Judaism, Christianity, and Islam are related traditions with their roots in the same part of the world. The Chinese tradition is quite distinct and, it is sometimes said, more focused on how one acts to those with whom one is in some relationship, especially familial; yet here, too, it is possible to find a very strong statement of our obligations to the poor. Mencius, who lived about three hundred years before the Christian era, is regarded as the most authoritative interpreter of the Confucian tradition, and in terms of his influence on Chinese thought is second only to Confucius himself. One of the works that describes his teachings recounts a visit he paid to the court of King Hui of Liang. On arriving, he met the king and said to him:

> There are people dying from famine on the roads, and you do not issue the stores of your granaries for them. When people die, you say, "It is not owing to me; it is owing to the year." In what does this differ from stabbing a man and killing him, and then saying "It was not I, it was the weapon?"[14]

There is nothing new about the idea that we have a strong moral obligation to help those in need. In one-on-one situations where rescue is easy, our intuitions tell us that it would be wrong not to do it. We all see or read appeals to help those living in extreme poverty in the world's poorest countries. And yet most of us reject the call to "do unto others." I'll turn now to some of the reasons we give for our failure to act.

3. Common Objections to Giving

You may think of yourself as a charitable person. Most Americans do, and the $306 billion they donated to charities in 2007, three quarters of which came directly from individuals, lends support to that belief. In the United States, charitable giving is around 2.2 percent of gross national income. That's significantly more than in any other country, and about double the level of charitable giving in most other rich nations. About seven in every ten households in the United States made some form of gift to charity in 2007.[1] Americans also give time: Nearly 30 percent do some kind of volunteer work, most with religious, educational, or community organizations, with the average amount given being about 50 hours a year. In contrast to financial donations, however, when it comes to volunteering, the United States lags behind several European nations, especially the Dutch, who give more than twice as much of their time. When financial donations and volunteering are combined, the United States ranks as the world's third most generous nation, behind the Netherlands and Sweden.[2]

But beneath these encouraging numbers is a slightly less encouraging picture, at least as concerns those who live in extreme poverty. According to "Giving USA 2008," the most authoritative report on U.S. charity, the largest portion of the money Americans give, fully a third of it, goes to religious institutions, where it pays for the salaries of the clergy and for building and maintaining churches, synagogues, and mosques. Some of that—but by the most optimistic estimate, less than 10 percent—is passed on as aid for developing countries. The next biggest sector is education, including universities, colleges, and libraries. Again, a small percentage of that goes toward scholarships to students from developing countries, or to fund research that can help reduce poverty and disease. "Giving USA 2008" lumps donations to international aid organizations together with gifts to other organizations that do not give aid to the poor but, for example, run international exchange programs or work for international peace and security. This entire category received only 4.3 percent of all American charitable giving. According to statistics from the Organisation for Economic Co-operation and Development (OECD), U.S. private philanthropy for foreign aid amounts to only 0.07 percent of the nation's gross national income (that's just 7 cents for every $100 of income).[3]

As someone who has chosen to read this book, you are probably among those who give to charity or who volunteer in their community; despite that, you may be less inclined to give a substantial portion of your income to save the lives of those living in extreme poverty in faraway places. Charity begins at home, the saying goes, and I've found that friends, colleagues, students, and lecture audiences express that resistance in various ways. I've seen it in columns, letters, and blogs too. Particularly interesting, because they reflect a line of thought prevalent in affluent America, were comments made by students taking an elective called Literature and Justice at Glennview High (that's not its real name), a school in a wealthy Boston suburb. As part of the reading for the course, teachers gave students an article that I wrote for *The New York Times* in

1999, laying out a version of the argument you have just read, and asked them to write papers in response.[4] Scott Seider, then a graduate student at Harvard University researching how adolescents think about obligations to others, interviewed thirty-eight students in two sections of the course and read their papers.[5]

Let's look at some of the objections raised by these varied sources. Perhaps the most fundamental objection comes from Kathryn, a Glennview student who believes we shouldn't judge people who refuse to give:

> *There is no black and white universal code for everyone. It is better to accept that everyone has a different view on the issue, and all people are entitled to follow their own beliefs.*

Kathryn leaves it to the individual to determine his or her moral obligation to the poor. But while circumstances do make a difference, and we should avoid being too black-and-white in our judgments, this doesn't mean we should accept that everyone is entitled to follow his or her own beliefs. That is moral relativism, a position that many find attractive only until they are faced with someone who is doing something really, really wrong. If we see a person holding a cat's paws on an electric grill that is gradually heating up, and when we vigorously object he says, "But it's fun, see how the cat squeals," we don't just say, "Oh, well, you are entitled to follow your own beliefs," and leave him alone. We can and do try to stop people who are cruel to animals, just as we stop rapists, racists, and terrorists. I'm not saying that failing to give is like committing these acts of violence, but if we reject moral relativism in some situations, then we should reject it everywhere.

After reading my essay, Douglas, another Glennview student, objected that I "should not have the right to tell people what to do." In one sense, he's correct about that. I've no right to tell you or anyone else what to do with your money, in the sense that that would imply that you *have* to do as I say. I've no authority over Douglas or over you. On the other hand, I do have the right of free speech, which I'm exercising right now by offering you some arguments you might consider before you decide what to do with your money. I hope that you will want to listen to a variety of views before making up your mind about such an important issue. If I'm wrong about that, though, you are free to shut the book now, and there's nothing I can do about it.

It's possible, of course, to think that morality is not relative, and that we should talk about it, but that the right view is that we aren't under any obligation to give anything at all. Lucy, another Glennview High student, wrote as follows:

> *If someone wants to buy a new car, they should. If someone wants to redecorate their house, they should, and if they need a suit, get it. They work for their money and they have the right to spend it on themselves.*

You've probably already had this thought: You've worked hard to get where you are now, so haven't you earned a right to enjoy it? This seems both fair and reflective of our basic economic values. Yet, when thinking about fairness, you might also consider that if you are a middle-class person in a developed country, you were fortunate to be born into social and economic circumstances that make it possible for you to live comfortably if you work hard and have the right abilities. In other places, you might have ended up poor, no matter how hard you worked. Warren Buffett, one of the world's richest people, acknowledged as much when he said: "If you stick me down in the middle of Bangladesh or Peru, you'll find out how much this talent is going to produce in the wrong kind of soil." Nobel Prize–winning economist and social scientist Herbert Simon estimated that "social capital" is responsible for at least 90 percent of what people earn in wealthy societies. Simon was talking about living in a society with good institutions, such as an efficient banking system, a police force that will protect you from criminals, and courts to which you can turn with reasonable hope of a just decision if someone breaches a contract with you. Infrastructure in the form of roads, communications, and a reliable power supply is also part of our social capital. Without these, you will struggle to escape poverty, no matter how hard you work. And most of the poor do work at least as hard as you. They have little choice, even though most people in rich nations would never tolerate the working conditions in poor countries. Work in poor countries is more likely to involve hard physical labor, because there are fewer machines to do the job; office workers in poor countries in the tropics rarely have the luxury of air-conditioning. If poor people are not working, it is likely because unemployment is higher in poor nations than in rich ones, and that is not the fault of the poor.

Lucy said that people have a right to spend the money they earn on themselves. Even if we agree with that, having a *right* to do something doesn't settle the question of what you *should* do. If you have a right to do something, I can't justifiably force you not to do it, but I can still tell you that you would be a fool to do it, or that it would be a horrible thing to do, or that you would be wrong to do it. You may have a right to spend your weekend surfing, but it can still be true that you ought to visit your sick mother. Similarly, we might say that the rich have a right to spend their money on lavish parties, Patek Philippe watches, private jets, luxury yachts, and space travel, or, for that matter, to flush wads of it down the toilet. Or that those of us with more modest means shouldn't be forced to forgo any of the less-expensive pleasures that offer us some relief from all the time we spend working. But we could still think that to choose to do these things rather than use the money to save human lives is wrong, shows a deplorable lack of empathy, and means that you are not a good person.

If we have the right to do as we wish with our money, that right would supply an objection to any attempt to force the rich to give their money away, or to attempts to take it from them, for example by taxation. I don't agree that we have such a right, but I am not arguing here for higher taxation or any other coercive means of increasing aid. I am talking about what we should *choose* to do with our money if we are to live ethically. At the same time, I'm not arguing against a governmental role in reducing global poverty. Whether governments should play such a role is simply a separate question from the argument I am making. My aim is to convince you, the individual reader, that you can and should be doing a lot more to help the poor.

Libertarians resist the idea that we have a duty to help others. Canadian philosopher Jan Narveson articulates that point of view:

> *We are certainly responsible for evils we inflict on others, no matter where, and we owe those people compensation . . . Nevertheless, I have seen no plausible argument that we owe something, as a matter of general duty, to those to whom we have done nothing wrong.*[6]

There is, at first glance, something attractive about the political philosophy that says: "You leave me alone, and I'll leave you alone, and we'll get along just fine." It appeals to the frontier mentality, to an ideal of life in the wide-open spaces where each of us can carve out our own territory and live undisturbed by the neighbors. At first glance, it seems perfectly reasonable. Yet there is a callous side to a philosophy that denies that we have any responsibilities to those who, through no fault of their own, are in need. Taking libertarianism seriously would require us to abolish all state-supported welfare schemes for those who can't get a job or are ill or disabled, and all state-funded health care for the aged and for those who are too poor to pay for their own health insurance. Few people really support such extreme views. Most think that we do have obligations to those we can help with relatively little sacrifice—certainly to those living in our own country, and I would argue that we can't justifiably draw the boundary there. But if I have not persuaded you of that, there is another line of argument to consider: If we have, in fact, been at least in part a cause of the poverty of the world's poorest people—if we are harming the poor—then even libertarians like Narveson will have to agree that we ought to compensate them.

Some people imagine that the wealth of the world is a static quantity, like a pie that must be divided among a lot of people. In that model, the bigger the slice the rich get, the less there is for the poor. If that really were how the world works, then a relatively small elite would be inflicting a terrible injustice on everyone else, for just 2 percent of the world's people own half the world's wealth, and the richest 10 percent own 85 percent of the wealth. In contrast, half the world's people have barely 1 percent of the world's assets to split among them.[7] But the world's wealth is not fixed in size. The world is vastly richer now than it was, say, a thousand years ago. By finding better ways to create what people want, entrepreneurs make themselves rich, but they don't necessarily make others poorer. This book is about absolute poverty, not about being poor relative to how wealthy your neighbors are; in absolute terms, entrepreneurs increase the world's wealth. So the unequal distribution of the world's wealth—startling though it is—is not sufficient to show that the rich have harmed the poor.

There are many ways in which it is clear, however, that the rich *have* harmed the poor. Ale Nodye knows about one of them. He grew up in a village by the sea, in Senegal, in West Africa. His father and grandfather were fishermen, and he tried to be one too. But after six years in which he barely caught enough fish to pay for the fuel for his boat, he set out by canoe for the Canary Islands, from where he hoped to become another of Europe's many illegal immigrants. Instead, he was arrested and deported. But he says he will try again, even though the voyage is dangerous and one of his cousins died on a similar trip. He has no choice, he says, because "there are no fish in the sea here anymore." A European Commission report shows that Nodye is right: The fish stocks from which Nodye's father and grandfather took their catch and fed their families have been destroyed by industrial fishing fleets that come from Europe, China, and Russia and sell their fish to well-fed Europeans who can afford to pay high prices. The industrial fleets drag vast nets across the seabed, damaging the coral reefs where fish breed. As a result, a major protein source for poor people has vanished, the boats are idle, and people who used to make a living fishing or building boats are unemployed. The story is repeated in many other coastal areas around the world.[8]

Or consider how we citizens of rich countries obtain our oil and minerals. Teodoro Obiang, the dictator of tiny Equatorial Guinea, sells most of his country's oil to American corporations, among them Exxon Mobil, Marathon, and Hess. Although his official salary is a modest $60,000, this ruler of a country of 550,000 people is richer than Queen Elizabeth II. He owns six private jets and a $35 million house in Malibu, as well as other houses in Maryland and Cape Town and a fleet of Lamborghinis, Ferraris, and Bentleys. Most of the people over whom he rules live in extreme poverty, with a life expectancy of forty-nine and an infant mortality of eighty-seven per one thousand (this means that more than one child in twelve dies before its first birthday).[9] Equatorial Guinea is an extreme case, but other examples are almost as bad. In 2005, the Democratic Republic of the Congo exported minerals worth $200 million. From this, its total tax revenues were $86,000. Someone was surely making money from these dealings, but not the people of the Congo.[10] In 2006, Angola made more than $30 billion in oil revenue, about $2,500 for each of its 12 million citizens. Yet the majority of Angolans have no access to basic health care; life expectancy is forty-one years; and one child in four dies before reaching the age of five. On Transparency International's corruption perception index, Angola is currently ranked 147th among 180 countries.

In their dealings with corrupt dictators in developing countries, international corporations are akin to people who knowingly buy stolen goods, with the difference that the international legal and political order recognizes the corporations not as criminals in possession of stolen goods but as the legal owners of the goods they have bought. This situation is, of course, profitable for corporations that do deals with dictators, and for us, since we use the oil, minerals, and other raw materials we need to maintain our prosperity. But for resource-rich developing countries, it is a disaster. The problem is not only the loss of immense wealth that, used wisely, could build the prosperity of the nation. Paradoxically, developing nations with rich deposits of oil or minerals are often worse off than otherwise comparable nations without those resources. One reason is that the revenue from the sale of the resources provides a huge financial incentive for anyone tempted to overthrow the government and seize power. Successful rebels know that if they succeed, they will be rewarded with immense personal wealth. They can also reward those who backed their coup, and they can buy enough arms to keep themselves in power no matter how badly they rule. Unless, of course, some of those to whom they give the arms are themselves tempted by the prospect of controlling all that wealth . . . Thus the resources that should benefit developing nations instead become a curse that brings corruption, coups, and civil wars.[11] If we use goods made from raw materials obtained by these unethical dealings from resource-rich but money-poor nations, we are harming those who live in these countries.

One other way in which we in the rich nations are harming

the poor has become increasingly clear over the past decade or two. President Yoweri Museveni of Uganda put it plainly, addressing the developed world at a 2007 meeting of the African Union: "You are causing aggression to us by causing global warming. . . . Alaska will probably become good for agriculture, Siberia will probably become good for agriculture, but where does that leave Africa?"[12]

Strong language, but the accusation is difficult to deny. Two-thirds of the greenhouse gases now in the atmosphere have come from the United States and Europe. Without those gases, there would be no human-induced global warming problem. Africa's contribution is, by comparison, extremely modest: less than 3 percent of the global emissions from burning fuel since 1900, somewhat more if land clearing and methane emissions from livestock production are included, but still a small fraction of what has been contributed by the industrialized nations. And while every nation will have some problems in adjusting to climate change, the hardship will, as Museveni suggests, fall disproportionately on the poor in the regions of the world closer to the equator. Some scientists believe that precipitation will decrease nearer the equator and increase nearer the poles. In any case, the rainfall upon which hundreds of millions rely to grow their food will become less reliable. Moreover, the poor nations depend on agriculture to a far greater degree than the rich. In the United States, agriculture represents only 4 percent of the economy; in Malawi it is 40 percent, and 90 percent of the population are subsistence farmers, virtually all of whom are dependent on rainfall. Nor will drought be the only problem climate change brings to the poor. Rising sea levels will inundate fertile, densely settled delta regions that are home to tens of millions of people in Egypt, Bangladesh, India, and Vietnam. Small Pacific Island nations that consist of low-lying coral atolls, like Kiribati and Tuvalu, are in similar danger, and it seems inevitable that in a few decades they will be submerged.[13]

The evidence is overwhelming that the greenhouse gas emissions of the industrialized nations have harmed, and are continuing to harm, many of the world's poorest people—along with many richer ones, too. If we accept that those who harm others must compensate them, we cannot deny that the industrialized nations owe compensation to many of the world's poorest people. Giving them adequate aid to mitigate the consequences of climate change would be one way of paying that compensation.

In a world that has no more capacity to absorb greenhouse gases without the consequence of damaging climate change, the philosophy of "You leave me alone, and I'll leave you alone" has become almost impossible to live by, for it requires ceasing to put any more greenhouse gases into the atmosphere. Otherwise, we simply are not leaving others alone.

America is a generous nation. As Americans, we are already giving more than our share of foreign aid through our taxes. Isn't that sufficient?

Asked whether the United States gives more, less, or about the same amount of aid, as a percentage of its income, as other wealthy countries, only one in twenty Americans gave the correct answer. When my students suggest that America is generous in this regard, I show them figures from the website of the OECD, on the amounts given by all the organization's donor members. They are astonished to find that the United States has, for many years, been at or near the bottom of the list of industrialized countries in terms of the proportion of national income given as foreign aid. In 2006, the United States fell behind Portugal and Italy, leaving Greece as the only industrialized country to give a smaller percentage of its national income in foreign aid. The average nation's effort in that year came to 46 cents of every $100 of gross national income, while the United States gave only 18 cents of every $100 it earned.

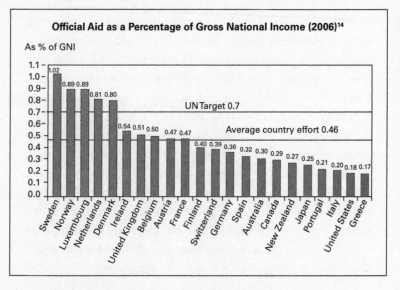

Official Aid as a Percentage of Gross National Income (2006)[14]

As % of GNI

In four different surveys that asked Americans what portion of government spending (not national income) goes to foreign aid, the median answers ranged from 15 percent to 20 percent. The correct answer is less than 1 percent.

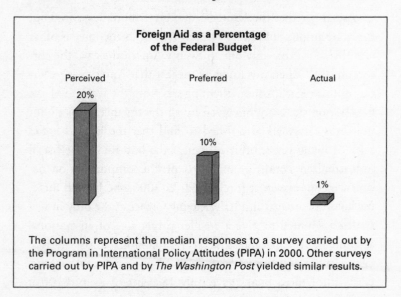

Foreign Aid as a Percentage of the Federal Budget

Perceived — 20%
Preferred — 10%
Actual — 1%

The columns represent the median responses to a survey carried out by the Program in International Policy Attitudes (PIPA) in 2000. Other surveys carried out by PIPA and by *The Washington Post* yielded similar results.

Asked what share of America's national income the United States gives in foreign aid, 42 percent of respondents believed that the nation gives more than four times as much as it actually gave, while 8 percent of Americans thought that the United States gives more than 100 times the actual amount![15]

A majority of people in these surveys also said that America gives too much aid—but when they were asked how much America should give, the median answers ranged from 5 percent to 10 percent of government spending. In other words, people wanted foreign aid "cut" to an amount five to ten times greater than the United States actually gives!

Some contend that these figures for official aid are misleading because America gives much more than other countries in private aid. But although the United States gives more private aid than most rich nations, even its private giving trails that of Australia, Canada, Ireland, and Switzerland as a percentage of national income, and is on a par with giving by people in Belgium and New Zealand. Adding U.S. nongovernmental aid, of 7 cents per $100 earned, to U.S. government aid leaves America's total aid contribution at no more than 25 cents of every $100 earned, still near the bottom of the international aid league.[16]

Philanthropic responses undermine real political change.

If those on the right fear that I am encouraging the state to seize their money and give it to the world's poor, some on the left worry that encouraging the rich to donate to aid organizations enables them to salve their consciences while they continue to benefit from a global economic system that makes them rich and keeps billions poor.[17] Philanthropy, philosopher Paul Gomberg believes, promotes "political quietism," deflecting attention from the institutional causes of poverty—

essentially, in his view, capitalism—and from the need to find radical alternatives to these institutions.[18]

Although I believe we ought to give a larger portion of our income to organizations combating poverty, I am open-minded about the best way to combat poverty.[19] Some aid agencies, Oxfam for example, are engaged in emergency relief, development aid, *and* advocacy work for a fairer global economic order. If, after investigating the causes of global poverty and considering what approach is most likely to reduce it, you really believe that a more revolutionary change is needed, then it would make sense to put your time, energy, and money into organizations promoting that revolution in the global economic system. But this is a practical question, and if there is little chance of achieving the kind of revolution you are seeking, then you need to look around for a strategy with better prospects of actually helping some poor people.

Giving people money or food breeds dependency.

I agree that we should not be giving money or food directly to the poor, except in emergencies like a drought, earthquake, or flood, where food may need to be brought in to stop people from starving in the short term. In less dire situations, providing food can make people dependent. If the food is shipped in from a developed nation, for example the United States, it can destroy local markets and reduce incentives for local farmers to produce a surplus to sell. We need to make it possible for people to earn their own money, or to produce their own food and meet their other needs in a sustainable manner and by their own work. Giving them money or food won't achieve that. Finding a form of aid that will really help people is crucial, and not a simple task, but as we'll see, it can be done.

Cash is the seed corn of capitalism. Giving it away will reduce future growth.

Gaetano Cipriano contacted me after reading one of my articles because he thought that as an entrepreneurial capitalist, he could offer a helpful perspective. The grandson of immigrants to America, he owns and runs EI Associates, an engineering and construction firm based in Cedar Knolls, New Jersey, that has assets of around $80 million. "Cash is the seed corn of capitalism" is his phrase. Gaetano told me that he deploys his capital to the best of his ability to promote profits and enduring growth, and that giving more of it away would be "cutting my own throat." But he does not spend extravagantly. "I do not live in a splendid house," he told me. "I have no second home. I drive a 2001 Ford Explorer with 73,000 miles. I belong to a nice squash club, and have four suits and two pairs of black shoes. When I take vacations they are short and local. I do not own a boat or a plane." While he does give to charity, he does it "at a level which is prudent and balanced with sustainable growth." If he were to give much more money away, it would have to come out of sums that he now reinvests in his business. That, in turn, would reduce his future earnings and perhaps the number of people he is able to employ, or how well he can pay them. It would also leave him with less to give if, later in life, he decides that he wants to give more.

For similar reasons, we can agree that it's a good thing Warren Buffett did not give away the first million dollars he earned. Had he done so, he would not have had the investment capital he needed to develop his business, and would never have been able to give away the $31 billion that he has now pledged to give. If you are as skilled as Buffett in investing your money, I urge you to keep it until late in life, too, and then give away most of it, as he has done. But people with less-spectacular investment abilities might do better to give it away sooner.

Claude Rosenberg, who died in 2008, was founder and chairman of RCM Capital Management, an institutional money management firm, so he knew something about investing, but he also knew a lot about philanthropy. He founded a group called New Tithing and wrote *Wealthy and Wise: How You and America Can Get the Most Out of Your Giving.* He argued that giving now is often a better value than investing your money and giving later, because the longer social problems are left unchecked, the worse they get. In other words, just as capital grows when invested, so the costs of fixing social problems are likely to grow. And, in Rosenberg's view, the rate at which the cost of fixing social problems grows is "exponentially greater" than the rate of return on capital.[20] In support of this belief, Rosenberg pointed to the cascading impact of poverty and other social problems, not just on one person but on future generations and society at large. The claim is a broad one, difficult to prove or disprove; but, if it is true for poverty in the United States, then it is even more likely to hold for poverty in developing countries, in part because it is easier to get a high percentage return when starting from a low base. Of course, that assumes that there are things we can do in developing countries that will be effective in reducing poverty.

What if you took every penny you ever had and gave it to the poor of Africa . . . ? What we would have is no economy, no ability to generate new wealth or help anybody.

This objection comes from Colin McGinn, a professor of philosophy at the University of Miami.[21] It isn't clear whether McGinn's "you" is you, the individual reader, or the group an American Southerner might refer to as "y'all." If you [insert your name], took every penny you ever had and gave it to the poor of Africa, our national economy would not notice. Even if every reader of this book did that, the economy would barely hiccup (unless the book's sales exceed my wildest dreams). If *everyone* in America did it, the national economy would be ruined. But, at the moment, there is no cause for worry about the last possibility: there is no sign of it happening, and I am not advocating it.

Because so few people give significant amounts, the need for more to be given is great, and the more each one of us gives, the more lives we can save. If everyone gave significantly more than they now give, however, we would be in a totally different situation. The huge gulf between rich and poor means that if everyone were giving, there would be no need for them to take every penny they ever had and give it all to Africa. As you'll see before the end of this book, quite a modest contribution from everyone who has enough to live comfortably, eat out occasionally, and buy bottled water, would suffice to achieve the goal of lifting most of the world's extremely poor people above the poverty line of $1.25 per day. If that modest contribution were given, we would no longer be in a situation in which 10 million children were dying from poverty every year. So whether a small number of people give a lot, or a large number of people give a little, ending large-scale extreme poverty wouldn't cripple our national economy. It leaves plenty of scope for entrepreneurial activity and individual wealth. In the long run, the global economy would be enhanced, rather than diminished, by bringing into it the 1.4 billion people now outside it, creating new markets and new opportunities for trade and investment.

People do have special relationships with their families, their communities, and their countries. This is the standard equipment of humanity, and most people, in all of human history, have seen nothing wrong with it.[22]

—Alan Ryan, philosopher and warden of New College, Oxford

It is true that most of us care more about our family and friends than we do about strangers. That's natural, and there is nothing wrong with it. But how far should preference for family and friends go? Brendan, a Glennview High student, thought that instead of going to aid for the poor, money "can be better spent helping your family and friends who need the money as well." If family and friends really *need* the money, in anything remotely like the way those living in extreme poverty need it, it would be going too much against the grain of human nature to object to giving to them before giving to strangers. Fortunately, most middle-class people in rich nations don't have to make this choice. They can take care of their families in an entirely sufficient way on much less than they are now spending, and thus have money left over that can be used to help those in extreme poverty. Admittedly, saying just where the balance should be struck is difficult. I'll return to that question later in the book.

Kiernan, another Glennview High School student, made a point similar to Alan Ryan's:

> *[Giving what we don't need to the poor] would make the world a better, more equal place. But it is like a little kid buying a pack of candy, keeping one piece, and giving the rest away. It just doesn't happen.*

The issue raised by all these remarks is the link between what we humans are (mostly) like, and what we *ought* to do. When Brendan O'Grady, a philosophy student at Queen's University in Ontario, posted a blog about this issue, he got the following response from another Canadian philosophy student Thomas Simmons:

> Of course I do not want people to die, but I just feel generally unattached to them. I have no doubt that if I were to take a trip to places where people are starving then I might think differently, but as it stands now they are just too far removed. In not making these donations, I am implicitly valuing the affluence of my own life over

the basic sustenance of many others. And, well, I guess I do. Am I immoral for doing so? Maybe.[23]

When O'Grady queried this, Simmons clarified his position: "I don't intend to make a moral defense, but rather just reveal my personal feelings—that is, just to explain how I feel." The distinction between describing how things are and saying how they ought to be is also relevant to what Kiernan and Alan Ryan are saying. The fact that we tend to favor our families, communities, and countries may explain our failure to save the lives of the poor beyond those boundaries, but it does not justify that failure from an ethical perspective, no matter how many generations of our ancestors have seen nothing wrong with it. Still, a good explanation of why we behave as we do is an important first step toward understanding to what extent change is possible.

HUMAN NATURE

4. Why Don't We Give More?

The world would be a much simpler place if one could bring about social change merely by making a logically consistent moral argument. But it's clear that even people who believe that they should give more don't always do so. We've learned a lot, in recent decades, about the psychological factors that lead people to behave in various ways. Now it's time to apply some of that knowledge to our problem: why people don't give more than they do, and what might lead them to give more.

If everyday life has not already convinced you that there is a human tendency to favor our own interests, psychologists have set up experiments to prove it. For example, Daniel Batson and Elizabeth Thompson gave participants in an experiment tasks to assign themselves and another participant, who was not present. One of the tasks was described as relatively interesting and included a significant benefit, while the other was described as boring and had no benefit. The participants were also told: "Most participants feel that giving both people an equal chance—by, for example, flipping a coin—is the fairest way to assign themselves and the other participant the tasks." A coin was provided for that purpose. Nobody except the participant could see how the coin fell. Interviewed after they had assigned the task, all of the participants said that the most moral response was either to flip the coin or to give the more rewarding task to the other participant. Yet about half chose not to flip the coin, and of those who did not use the coin, more than 80 percent gave themselves the more rewarding task. More remarkably, however, it seems that on 85 percent of the occasions when the coin was tossed, it landed on the side that assigned the more rewarding task to the person who tossed it![1]

Yet we often do kind and generous things. The medical services of most developed nations rely for their blood supply on the altruism of ordinary citizens who donate their own blood to strangers. They give up their time and go through having a needle inserted in a vein—an experience many find unsettling—for no reward except perhaps a cup of indifferent coffee or tea. They don't even get priority if they should need blood themselves. And when people say without the slightest hesitation that they would save the drowning child, they are probably telling the truth. So why don't we save children in developing countries, if the cost of doing so is modest? Beyond the simple battle between selfishness and altruism, other psychological factors are at work, and in this chapter I will describe six of the most important.

The Identifiable Victim

Researchers seeking to find out what triggers generous responses paid participants in a psychological experiment and then gave them the opportunity to donate some of the money to Save the Children, an organization that helps children in poverty both in the United States and in developing countries. One group was given general information about the need for donations, including statements like "Food shortages in

Malawi are affecting more than three million children." A second group was shown the photo of a seven-year-old Malawian girl named Rokia; they were told that Rokia is desperately poor and that "her life will be changed for the better by your gift."

The group receiving information about Rokia gave significantly more than the group receiving only general information. Then a third group was given the general information, the photo, and the information about Rokia. That group gave more than the group that had received only the general information, but still gave less than the group that had received *only* the information about Rokia.[2] Indeed, even adding a second identifiable child to the information about Rokia— while providing no general information—led to a lower average donation than when only one child was mentioned. The subjects of the experiment reported feeling stronger emotions when told about one child than when told about two children.[3]

Another study produced a similar result. One group of people was told that a single child needed lifesaving medical treatment that costs $300,000. A second group was told that eight children would die unless they were given treatment that could be provided for all of them at a total cost of $300,000. Again, those told about the single child gave more.[4]

This "identifiable victim effect" leads to "the rule of rescue": we will spend far more to rescue an identifiable victim than we will to save a "statistical life." Consider the case of Jessica McClure, who was eighteen months old in 1987 when she fell into a dry well in Midland, Texas. As rescuers worked for two and a half days to reach her, CNN broadcast images of the rescue to millions of viewers around the world. Donors sent in so much money that Jessica now has what has been reported to be a million-dollar trust fund.[5] Elsewhere in the world, unnoticed by the media and not helped by the money

donated to Jessica, about 67,500 children died from avoidable poverty-related causes during those two and a half days according to UNICEF. Yet it was obvious to everyone involved
that Jessica must be rescued, no matter what the cost. Similarly, we do not abandon trapped miners or lost sailors, even
though we could save more lives by using the money spent
on such rescues on making dangerous intersections safer.
In providing health care, too, we will spend much more trying to save a particular patient, often in vain, than promoting
preventive measures that would save many people from becoming ill.[6]

The identifiable person moves us in a way that more-
abstract information does not. But the phenomenon doesn't
even require particular details about the person. People asked
by researchers to make a donation to Habitat for Humanity in
order to house a needy family were told either that the family
"has been selected" or that the family "will be selected." In
every other detail, the wording of the request was the same. In
neither case were the subjects told who the family was, or
would be, nor were they given any other information about the
family. Yet the group told that the family had already been selected gave substantially more. [7]

Paul Slovic, a leading researcher in this field, believes that the
identifiable—or even predetermined—person appeals to us so
much because we use two distinct processes for grasping reality
and deciding what to do: the affective system and the deliberative system.[8] The affective system is grounded in our emotional
responses. It works with images, real or metaphorical, and with
stories, rapidly processing them to generate an intuitive feeling
that something is right or wrong, good or bad. That feeling
leads to immediate action. The deliberative system draws on our
reasoning abilities, rather than our emotions, and it works with
words, numbers, and abstractions rather than with images and
stories. These processes are conscious, and they require us to ap-
praise logic and evidence. As a result, the deliberative system

takes a little longer than the affective system, and does not result in such immediate action.

An individual in need tugs at our emotions. That's our affective system at work. Mother Teresa expressed this when she said: "If I look at the mass I will never act. If I look at the one, I will."[9] If we pause to think about it, we know that "the mass" is made up of individuals, each with needs as pressing as "the one," and our reason tells us that it is better to act to help that individual *plus* an additional individual than to help just the one, and even better to help those two individuals *plus* a third individual, and so on. We know that our deliberative system is right, yet for Mother Teresa as for many others, this knowledge lacks the impact of something that tugs on our emotions the way a single needy person does.

More evidence about the distinctive ways in which these two systems work comes from some more-complicated experiments carried out by the same team that did the experiments comparing the responses of people given information about a "Rokia" with those given more general information. This time the researchers were investigating whether arousing the emotions of the research subjects led them to respond differently to the two kinds of information. Once again, the participants all completed a standard survey, and then one randomly selected group was given emotionally neutral questions (for example, math puzzles) while the other group was given questions designed to arouse their emotions (for example, "When you hear the word 'baby,' what do you feel?"). Then everyone was given the opportunity to donate some of their payment for the experiment to a charity, but for half of each group the information included Rokia only, while the other half was given the more general information about people in need. Those who had answered the emotionally arousing questions and received the information about Rokia gave almost twice as much as those who got the same information but had responded to the emotionally neutral questions.

But the amount given by those who received the general information was not significantly affected by the questions they had answered. Our response to the images and stories—and thus to identifiable victims—is dependent on our emotions, but our response to more-abstract facts, conveyed in words and numbers, remains much the same whatever the state of our emotions.[10]

Parochialism

Two hundred and fifty years ago, philosopher and economist Adam Smith invited his readers to reflect on their attitudes to distant strangers by asking them to imagine that "the great empire of China, with all its myriads of inhabitants, was suddenly swallowed up by an earthquake." Consider, he then asked his readers, "how a man of humanity in Europe," who had no special connection with that part of the world, would receive the news. Whatever that person might say, Smith contends, "he would pursue his business or his pleasure, take his repose or his diversion, with the same ease and tranquillity, as if no such accident had happened."[11]

The tragic earthquake that struck China's Sichuan province in 2008 showed only too clearly that Smith's observation still holds. Though the earthquake killed 70,000 people, injured 350,000, and made nearly 5 million homeless, its impact on me was quite temporary. Reading about the deaths and seeing the devastation on television aroused my sympathy for the families of the victims, but I did not stop work, lose sleep, or even cease to enjoy the normal pleasures of life. No one I knew did. Our intellect—our deliberative system—takes in the news of the disaster, but our emotions are rarely disturbed by tragedies that occur to strangers far away with whom we have no special connection. Even if we are moved to donate to emergency relief, hearing such terrible news does not change our lives in any fundamental way.

At our best, we give far less to help foreigners than we give to those within our own country. The tsunami that struck Southeast Asia just after Christmas 2004, killed 220,000 people and rendered millions homeless and destitute. It prompted Americans to give $1.54 billion for disaster relief work, the largest amount that Americans have ever given after any natural disaster outside the United States. But it was less than a quarter of the $6.5 billion Americans gave the following year to help those affected by Hurricane Katrina, which killed about 1,600 people and left far fewer homeless than the tsunami. An earthquake in Pakistan in October 2005 that killed 73,000 people elicited a comparatively small $150 million in donations from Americans. (The earthquake was the only one of these three tragic events that was not caught on video and so did not result in dramatic and oft-repeated television coverage.) Bear in mind that the victims of the American disasters were also being helped by a government with far greater resources than the governments of the countries struck by the tsunami and the earthquake.[12]

Discomforting as our relative indifference to foreigners may be, it is easy to understand why we are like this. Our species has spent millions of years evolving as social mammals with offspring who need their parents' care for many years. For most of these millions of years, parents who did not care for their children during this period of dependence were unlikely to pass on their genes.[13] Hence our concern for the welfare of others tends to be limited to our kin, and to those with whom we are in cooperative relationships, and perhaps to members of our own small tribal group.

Even when nation-states formed and tribal ethics began to be constricted by the requirements of the larger society, the intuition that we should help others usually extended only to helping our compatriots. In *Bleak House*, Charles Dickens lends his support to parochialism by ridiculing the "telescopic philanthropy" of Mrs. Jellyby, who "could see nothing nearer than Africa." She works hard on a project that will educate the natives of Borrioboola-Gha, on the left bank of the Niger, but her house is a mess and her children are neglected.[14] It was easy for Dickens to make fun of Mrs. Jellyby, for such philanthropy was, in his day, misguided. It was hard to know whether people far away needed our help; if they did, it was even harder to find effective ways of helping them. Anyway, there were many British poor in circumstances scarcely less desperate. In noting the limits to our sympathy for those far away, Adam Smith said that this state of affairs "seems wisely ordered by Nature," since those far from us are people "we can neither serve nor hurt." If we cared more, it would "produce only anxiety to ourselves, without any manner of advantage to them."[15] Today these words are as obsolete as the quill with which Smith wrote them. As our response to the tsunami vividly demonstrated, instant communications and rapid transport mean that we *can* help those far from us in ways that were impossible in Smith's day. In addition, the gap between the living standards of people in developed nations and those in developing nations has increased enormously, so that those living in industrialized nations have greater capacity to help those far away, and greater reason to focus our aid on them: far away is where the vast majority of the extremely poor are.

Futility

In one study, people were told that there were several thousand refugees at risk in a camp in Rwanda and were asked how willing they were to send aid that would save the lives of 1,500 of them. In asking this question, the researchers varied the total number of people they said were at risk, but kept the number that the aid would save at 1,500. People turned out to be more willing to send aid that saved 1,500 out of 3,000 people at risk than they were to send aid that saved 1,500 out of 10,000 at risk. In general, the smaller the proportion of people at risk who can be saved, the less willing people are to send aid.[16] We seem to respond as if anything that leaves most of the people in the camp at risk is "futile"—although, of course, for the 1,500 who will be saved by the aid, and for their families and friends, the rescue is anything but futile, irrespective of the total number in the camp. Paul Slovic, who coauthored this study, concludes that "the *proportion* of lives saved often carries more weight than the *number* of lives saved." The implication is that people will give more support for saving 80 percent of 100 lives at risk than for saving 20 percent of 1,000 lives at risk—in other words, for saving 80 lives rather than for saving 200 lives, even when the cost of saving each group is the same.[17]

The high school students introduced in the previous chapter said things like "It's going to go on" and "There will never be enough money to help all these people." Many of us engage in what psychologists label "futility thinking." We say that aid to the poor is "drops in the ocean," implying that it is not worth giving, because no matter how much we do, the ocean of people in need will seem just as vast as it was before.

The Diffusion of Responsibility

We are also much less likely to help someone if the responsibility for helping does not rest entirely on us. In a famous case that jolted the American psyche, Kitty Genovese, a young woman in Queens, New York, was brutally attacked and killed while thirty-eight people in different apartments reportedly saw or heard what was happening but did nothing to aid her. The revelation that so many people heard Genovese's screams, but failed even to pick up the phone to call the police, led to a national debate about "what kind of people we have become."*

The public debate that followed the Kitty Genovese murder led psychologists John Darley and Bib Latané to explore the phenomenon of diffusion of responsibility. They invited students to participate in a market research survey. The students went to an office, where they were met by a young woman who told them to sit down and gave them some questionnaires to fill out. She then went into an adjacent room separated from the office only by a curtain. After a few minutes, the students heard noises suggesting that she had climbed on a chair to get something from a high shelf, and the chair had fallen over. She cried out: "Oh, my God, my foot . . ." "I . . . I . . . can't move . . . it. Oh, my ankle. I . . . can't . . . can't . . . get . . . this thing off . . . me." The moaning and crying went on for about another minute.[19] Of those students who were alone in the adjoining room filling out the market research survey, 70 percent offered to help. When another person who appeared to be a student completing the survey—but was in fact a stooge—was also present, and that person did not respond to the calls for help, only 7 percent offered to help. Even when two genuine students were together in the room, the proportion offering to help was much lower than when there was only one student. The diffusion of responsibility had a marked inhibiting effect—the "bystander effect." Other experiments have yielded similar results.[20]

---

*Long after the name "Kitty Genovese" had become a byword for the indifference of big-city residents to their neighbors, a more thorough investigation raised serious doubts about the initial reports, specifically about how many witnesses really knew what was happening and had the opportunity to report it.[18]

The Sense of Fairness

Nobody likes being the only one cleaning up while everyone else stands around. In the same way, our willingness to help the poor can be reduced if we think that we would be doing more than our fair share. The person considering giving a substantial portion of his or her disposable income can't help but be aware that others, including those with a lot more disposable income, are not. Imagine writing that first big check for UNICEF or Oxfam, and then running into your neighbors coming back from a winter vacation in the Caribbean, looking relaxed and tanned, and telling you about their great adventures sailing and scuba diving. How would you feel?

So strong is our sense of fairness that, to prevent others getting more than their fair share, we are often willing to take less for ourselves. In the "ultimatum game," two players are told that one of them, the proposer, will be given a sum of money, say $10, and must divide it with the second player, the responder, but *how* the money is divided is up to the proposer, who can offer as much or as little as she wishes. If the responder rejects the offer, neither will get anything. The game is played only once, and the players' identities are not revealed, so their decisions will not be influenced by any thoughts of payback if they should meet again. If the players acted purely from self-interest, the proposer would offer the smallest possible amount and the responder would accept it, because after all, even a little is better than nothing at all. But in many different cultures, most proposers offer an equal split of the money. That offer is invariably accepted. Occasionally, however, proposers behave as economists would expect them to, and offer less than 20 percent. Then most responders confound the economists by rejecting the offer.[21] Even monkeys will reject a reward for a task if they see another monkey getting a better reward for performing the same task.[22]

Responders who reject small offers show that even when dealing with a complete stranger with whom they will never interact again, they would rather punish unfairness than gain money. Why would people (and monkeys) act in ways that seem contrary to their own interest? The most plausible answer is that moral intuitions like fairness developed because they enhanced the reproductive fitness of those who had them and the groups to which they belonged. Among social animals, those who form cooperative relationships tend to do much better than those who do not. By making a fair offer, you signal that you are the kind of person who would make a good partner for cooperating. Conversely, by rejecting an unfair offer, you show that you are not going to put up with getting a raw deal, and thus you deter others from trying to take advantage of you. There are also social advantages to such intuitions. A society in which most people act fairly will generally do better than one in which everyone is always seeking to take unfair advantage, because people will be better able to trust each other and form cooperative relationships.

Money

Are we less likely to respond to the needs of others if the only way to respond is to send money? We already know that the lack of an identifiable individual lengthens the odds against our helping. But is it possible that the fact that money is often the only feasible means of helping the distant poor also reduces our willingness to help those we cannot reach?

If you have ever read Karl Marx, you will not be surprised at the idea that the use of money undermines what is best and noblest in human relationships. In *The Economic and Philosophical Manuscripts of 1844,* a youthful work that remained unpublished and largely unknown until the mid-twentieth century, Marx describes money as "the universal agent of separation" because it transforms human characteristics and powers into something else. As an example, he suggested, a man may be ugly, but if he has money, he can buy for himself "the most beautiful of women." Money alienates us, Marx thought, from our true human nature and from our fellow human beings.

If we had only Marx's authority for this view, we could dismiss it as ideologically motivated. But a report in *Science* by Kathleen Vohs, Nicole Mead, and Miranda Goode, who work in marketing and psychology, and display no awareness that Marx had anything to say about their topic, suggests that on this point, at least, Marx was on to something.

Vohs and her colleagues conducted a series of experiments that involved priming subjects to think about money. They gave them tasks that involved unscrambling phrases about money, or they placed piles of Monopoly money nearby, or they ensured that the subjects saw a screen saver with various denominations of money. Other subjects, randomly selected, unscrambled phrases that were not about money, did not see Monopoly money, and saw different screen savers. In each case, those who had been primed to think about money—let's call them the "money group"—behaved in ways that showed greater distance from others and more self-sufficiency. The money group

- Took longer to ask for help when engaged in a difficult task and told that help was available
- Left a greater distance between chairs when told to move their chair so they could talk with another participant
- Were more likely to choose a leisure activity that could be enjoyed alone than one that involved others
- Were less helpful to others

- When invited to donate some of the money they had been paid for participation in the experiment, gave less

The researchers were struck by how great a difference the trivial reminders of money made. For example, where the control group offered to spend an average of forty-two minutes helping someone with a task, those primed to think about money offered only twenty-five minutes. Similarly, when someone pretending to be another participant in the experiment asked for help, the money group spent only half as much time helping her. When asked to make a donation, the money group gave just a little over half as much as the control group.[23]

Why does money make us less willing to seek or give help, and to be close to others? Vohs and her colleagues suggest that as societies began to use money, the need to rely on family and friends diminished, and people were able to become more self-sufficient. "In this way," they conclude, "money enhanced individualism but diminished communal motivations, an effect that is still apparent in people's responses today." British social scientist Richard Titmuss made a similar point nearly forty years ago, in response to the tide of economic opinion then flowing in favor of allowing blood to be bought and sold for medical purposes. Most economists took the view that the best way to obtain an adequate supply of any commodity is to allow the laws of supply and demand to set the price. British law prohibited the sale of blood, relying on voluntary, altruistic donations, and thus interfering with the laws of supply and demand. In *The Gift Relationship,* Titmuss defended this system on the grounds that it strengthened ties of community. If blood is literally priceless, we all must rely, in a medical emergency, on the lifesaving gifts of strangers. And anyone, no matter how rich or poor, can give back to the community by offering the gift of life to strangers in need. Once you allow blood to be bought and sold, it becomes a commodity and there is no need for altruism, because if there are not enough altruistic donors, blood can be bought.[24]

Psychology, Evolution, and Ethics

To many, the intuitions discussed in this chapter amount to a reasonable rejoinder, gathered under the general notion "It's not in our nature," to arguments for the moral necessity to give to the distant poor. And, at first glance, the moral judgment that we should help the victim we can see over the victim we can't feels right. If we think again, however, the intuition doesn't stand up to examination. Suppose that we are in a boat in a storm and we see two capsized yachts. We can either rescue one person clinging to one upturned yacht, or five people who we cannot see, but we know are trapped inside the other upturned yacht. We will have time to go to only one of the yachts before they are pounded onto the rocks and, most likely, anyone clinging to the yacht we do not go to will be drowned. We can identify the man who is alone—we know his name and what he looks like, although otherwise we know nothing about him and have no connection with him. We don't know anything about who is trapped inside the other yacht, except that there are five of them. If we have no reason to think that the single identifiable victim is in any way more worthy of rescue than each of the five nonidentifiable people, surely we should rescue the larger number of people. What's more, if we put ourselves in the position of the people needing to be rescued— but without knowing which of the six we are—we would want the rescuers to go to the capsized yacht with five people, because that will give us the best chance of being rescued.

The same is true for each of the other five psychological factors we have investigated. Our parochial feelings are a restriction on our willingness to act on our capacity, both financial and technological, to give to those beyond the borders of our nation and thereby to do much more good than we can do if our philanthropy stops at those borders. Bill Gates, the master of global technology, has drawn the implications for ethics of the fact that we are now one world. His philanthropy is primarily focused on doing the most good in the world as a whole. When asked by an interviewer for *Forbes* what advice he'd offer the next U.S. president to improve American competitiveness and innovation, Gates batted the question straight back, saying: "I tend to think more about improving the entire world as opposed to relative positions. Otherwise you could say, 'Hey, World War Two was great because the U.S. was in its strongest relative position when that was over.' "[25]

Even less defensible than parochialism are the feelings of futility that lead us to focus on the number of people we cannot help, rather than the number we can. The "drops in the ocean" response to the argument for giving aid overlooks the fact that my aid will help specific individuals, families, or even villages, and the good that I do for them is not lessened by the fact that there are many more needy people I cannot help.

Others find intuitive appeal in the diffusion of responsibility. Thus they believe that I have a stronger obligation to save the drowning child than to give aid to the poor, because I am the only person in a position to save the child, whereas there are a billion people in a position to save the 10 million children dying annually from poverty-related causes. But even though a billion others *could* help the children who will be helped by your donation, what difference does that make if you know that they won't, or anyway that not enough of them will for all of those 10 million children to be saved?

Patterns of behavior that helped our ancestors survive and reproduce may, in today's very different circumstances, be of no benefit to us or to our descendants. Even if some evolved intuition or way of acting were still conducive to our survival and reproduction, however, that would not, as Darwin himself recognized, make it right. Evolution has no moral direction. An evolutionary understanding of human nature can explain the differing intuitions we have when we are faced with an individual rather than with a mass of people, or with people close to us rather than with those far away, but it does not justify those feelings.

But of course, concluding that others' needs should count as much as our own is not the same as feeling it, and that is the core of the problem of why we do not respond to the needs of the world's poorest people as we would respond to someone in need of rescue right in front of us.[26] Skeptics doubt that reason has any influence on whether we act ethically. It's all a matter of what we want, or desire, they say, of what feels good or bad to us, of what we find attractive or repugnant. They deny that understanding or argument—in a word, the kind of thing that philosophers write, and of which this book largely consists—is ever going to lead anyone to action. Here is one small piece of evidence to counter that. In the same *New York Times* piece about global poverty that the Glennview High School students read, I included telephone numbers that readers could call to donate to UNICEF or Oxfam America. These organizations later told me that in the month after the article appeared, those phone lines brought in about $600,000 more than they usually took in. Now that's not a vast sum, given how many people read *The New York Times* on Sundays. Still, it does mean that the article persuaded a significant number of people to give. Some of those donors have continued to do so. Several years after the article was published, I have been told, someone came to the Oxfam office in Boston, took a carefully preserved copy of my article out of her bag, and told the staff that she had been meaning to give to the organization ever since reading it. She has since become a major donor. My knowledge of the impact that this kind of work can have has been a powerful reason for writing this book.

Now let's look at some of those who do respond to appeals to give, and ask what we can do to encourage others to respond in the same way.

5. Creating a Culture of Giving

Thirty years ago, Chris Ellinger received the phone call that changed his life. It was from a stockbroker offering him advice on his portfolio. The call seemed strange, because Chris had very little money. It turned out that the stockbroker had managed to learn even before he did that his grandmother had left him $250,000. But what to do with all that money? Chris was then living with a community of people working for social justice in Philadelphia, so he was well aware that he was more fortunate than others. Why should he be wealthy, he asked himself, when so many were poor? He soon started giving away between a third and half of the income from his new investments. He thought about giving away much more, but he was also afraid of giving away "too much," although he only had a vague idea what that might mean. More than was reasonable? More than was prudent? More than most people gave? He approached other members of his family about what they gave away, but no one seemed to want to talk about it.

Eight years later, Chris was at a conference of philanthropists when a woman spoke up and asked whether anyone in the room had seriously considered giving away large portions of their wealth. A few people, including Chris, raised their hands. Before long, four of them began meeting to talk about giving away not only their income, but most of their capital. With each other's support, they began to give away even more than they had in the past. Three of them gave away more than half their wealth. Thus began the 50% League, which by 2008 had more than a hundred members, some wealthy, others of modest means. To qualify, they must have given away at least half their wealth, or, for each of the past three years, half their income.

The 50% League shows that with the right support from like-minded friends, some people will do much more than we would have believed possible—more, even, than they themselves believed they could give. Without expecting more than a tiny minority to give as much as half their wealth or income, it is worth asking what can be done to create a culture of giving that can combat the various elements of human psychology that, as we saw in the last chapter, make us less likely to help the distant poor.

Getting It into the Open

If our sense of fairness makes us less likely to give when others are not doing so, the converse also holds: we are much more likely to do the right thing if we think others are already doing it.[1] More specifically, we tend to do what others in our "reference group"—those with whom we identify—are doing.[2] And studies show that the amount people give to charity is related to how much they believe others are giving. Psychologists Jen Shang and Rachel Croson used a funding drive from an American public radio station to test whether the amount that callers donated varied when the person answering the call mentioned that a recent caller had donated a particular sum. They found that mentioning a figure close to the upper end of what callers generally gave—to be precise, at the ninetieth percentile—resulted in callers donating substantially more than a control group not provided with this information. The effect was surprisingly enduring: Donors who were told about another member's above-average contribution were twice as likely to renew their membership a year later. Those receiving this information by mail reacted in roughly the same way.[3]

Jesus told us not to sound a trumpet when we give to the poor, "as the hypocrites do in the synagogues and in the streets, so that they may be honored by men." Instead, he advised, we should give so secretly that not even our left hand knows what our right hand is doing. Only then would we be rewarded in heaven, rather than on earth.[4] Indeed, many of us believe that if people are motivated only by a desire to "be honored by men" or to improve their reputation for generosity, they are not *really* being generous, and will not be generous when no one is looking. Similarly, today when people give large sums with a lot of fanfare, we suspect that their real motive is to gain social status by their philanthropy, and to draw attention to how rich and generous they are. But does this really matter? Isn't it more important that the money go to a good cause than that it be given with "pure" motives? And if by sounding a trumpet when they give, they encourage others to give, that's better still.

Jesus was not the only one to favor anonymous donors. The twelfth-century Jewish thinker Maimonides drew up a celebrated "ladder of charity" in which he ranked different ways of giving alms. For Maimonides, it was important that the recipient not feel indebted to the donor, or be publicly humiliated by the need to accept charity. Hence giving when either the donor is known to the recipient or the recipient is known to the donor ranks lower than giving anonymously and without knowing the recipient of the gift. Almsgiving then was local: The donor and the recipient lived in the same community and probably crossed paths in daily life. But in an age of global philanthropy, the risk of the recipient being burdened by a feeling of indebtedness to a particular donor is less significant, and it is outweighed by the importance of developing a culture of giving.

Admittedly, the desire to get one's name on something can be taken to extremes, as the *New York Times* theater critic Charles Isherwood observed when he attended the opening performance at the new home of the Shakespeare Theatre Company in Washington, D.C. The building is called Sidney Harman Hall, but the naming doesn't stop there:

> You enter through the Arlene and Robert Kogod Lobby. From there you may choose to ascend to the orchestra level by taking either the Morris and Gwendolyn Cafritz Foundation Grand Staircase West or the Philip L. Graham Fund Grand Staircase East. . . . Should you arrive with time for a drink before the curtain, you can linger near the James and Esthy Adler Orchestra Terrace West, or the less personal-sounding American Airlines Orchestra Terrace East. And don't forget to check your bulky outerwear at the Cassidy & Associates Coat Room, before entering the Landon and Carol Butler Theater Stage to watch the performance.[5]

Isherwood laments that this "philanthropic graffiti" cuts against the "ideally selfless spirit" of giving in order to provide a public good. (One might, of course, wonder why people with an ideally selfless spirit would be giving millions for a grand new theater in the capital of one of the world's wealthiest nations anyway, but that would be a subversive thought for a theater critic.) In any case, since we know that people will give more if they believe that others are giving more, we should not worry too much about the motives with which they give.

Rather, we should encourage them to be more open about the size of their donations. Those who make it known that they give a significant portion of what they earn can increase the likelihood that others will do the same. If these others also talk about it, the long-term effect will be amplified, and over a decade or two, the amount given will rise.

That is the kind of change Chris Ellinger sought to effect when, together with his wife, Anne, he launched the 50% League. They and other members of the league wanted to get their giving out into the open, in order to inspire others and change expectations about what is a "normal" or "reasonable" amount to give. To further that goal, their website publicizes members' stories. Here are a few, more or less randomly chosen from the website.

- Annie Bennett takes $28,000 a year from her small business and gives the remaining $30,000 in profits to Prevent Child Abuse America.

- Tom Hsieh and his wife, Bree, made a commitment to living on less than the U.S. median income, currently $46,000 a year. In 2006, they and their one-year-old daughter lived on $38,000. As Hsieh, who is thirty-six, earns more, they give more away, mostly to Christian organizations helping the poor in developing countries. Hsieh says that whether or not his giving has saved the lives of others, it has saved his own: "I could easily have lived a life that was boring and inconsequential. Now I am graced with a life of service and meaning."

- For the past thirteen years, Hal Taussig and his wife have given away almost all their business profits, about $3 million. Now, Taussig writes, "living happily on our Social Security checks gives us the slack to give away more." When people praise him for his generosity, he tells them: "Frankly, it's my own way of getting kicks out of life."

- When he was twenty-five, Chuck Collins, a grandson of the meatpacker Oscar Mayer, gave his inheritance to foundations promoting social change. That was more than twenty years ago. The cofounder of an organization called Responsible Wealth, Collins believes that inherited wealth is bad for children and bad for society. Responsible Wealth has been a leader in efforts to persuade the U.S. Congress not to abolish the estate tax.

- Tom White could have been among the superrich, because his father founded a highly successful construction business; Tom built it into the largest in Boston. But in 1983, he met Paul Farmer, then still a student at Harvard Medical School, who had already started a one-room clinic in Haiti. Inspired by Farmer's personal dedication to the poor, White has given "tens of millions" of dollars to Farmer's organization, Partners in Health, helping it provide health care for the rural poor in Haiti and Peru. He considers it "sinful to sit on millions when you know people are starving."

- John Hunting is still rich by most people's standards, although he has given away at least 50 percent of his income for the past thirty years, and 100 percent for the last ten. His father cofounded Steelcase, the world's largest manufacturer of office equipment. When the company went public in 1998, Hunting found himself with stock worth $130 million. He started a foundation, the Beldon Fund, aimed at bringing about a healthy and sustainable planet, and endowed it with $100 million. He plans to give away the rest of his inheritance by 2010.[6]

Putting a Face on the Needy

To tap into our greater willingness to help people who are identifiable, the British group Foster Parents Plan linked poor children in developing countries with "foster parents" in affluent nations who sent the child money for food, clothing, and education. In return, they received letters from "their" child. This approach avoided five of the six psychological barriers to aiding the poor mentioned above. In addition to the fact that the foster parents were helping an identifiable child, they knew that their aid was not futile, because they got letters from the child telling them what a difference it made, and they were not focused on other needy children they were unable to help. Their responsibility for "their" child was very clear: If they stopped donating, the child might have to go without food, clothing, or education, because there was no guarantee that anyone else would step in to help that particular child. Their sense of fairness was satisfied, because they were supporting just one child, generally not an especially onerous burden, and they knew that many other people were doing the same. And although the child was far away, the idea that they were the child's "foster parents" made the child part of their family and helped overcome the barrier of parochialism. The one barrier that couldn't be overcome was that the only way the foster parents could assist the child was by giving money.

This seems as close as possible to an ideal arrangement for tapping into the feelings of affluent people so that they will help the poor in distant countries. But it comes at a cost, because giving money to individual children isn't a particularly effective way of helping the poor. It doesn't assist families in providing for themselves, and it can lead to envy and dissension if some children get money and others don't. Problems like the lack of safe drinking water, sanitation, and health care can be addressed only by projects undertaken at the level of the community rather than the family. Foster Parents Plan, to its credit, realized this. It renamed itself Plan International and shifted to a more community-based approach. It does its best to retain the appeal of the identifiable child by continuing to invite potential donors to "Sponsor a Child" for between £12 and £17 ($24 to $34) per month, and the sponsors can write and receive letters, visit their sponsor child, and send "small gifts." But potential sponsors are also told: "Your money does not go to the individual child that you sponsor. So that Plan can make efficient use of funds, the money is pooled with contributions from other sponsors to support programs benefiting communities worldwide."[7]

The Right Kind of Nudge

Understanding human behavior has made it possible for some countries to achieve dramatic increases in the rate of organ donation. Could this be applied to giving to the poor as well? In Germany, only 12 percent of the population is registered to become organ donors if as a result of an accident they should be declared brain-dead. In Austria, the comparable figure is an astonishing 99.98 percent. Germans and Austrians are not so different in their cultural backgrounds, so why should Austrians be so much more willing to donate their organs? They probably are not. The difference is explained by the fact that in Germany you must put yourself on the register to become a potential organ donor, while in Austria you are a potential organ donor unless you object. The same pattern applies across Europe. In four countries with "opt in" systems, the *highest* proportion of registered donors, even after extensive public-relations campaigns, is 27.5 percent. In seven countries with "opt out" systems, the *lowest* proportion of potential donors is 85.9 percent.[8] Just as we tend to leave unchanged the factory settings on a computer, so other kinds of "defaults" can make a

big difference to our behavior—and, in the case of organ donations, save thousands of lives.

There is a new wave of interest in exploring how to frame
choices so that people make better decisions. Richard Thaler
and Cass Sunstein, professors of economics and law, respec-
tively, teamed up to write *Nudge: Improving Decisions About
Health, Wealth, and Happiness,* which advocates using defaults
to nudge us to make better choices.[9] Even when we are choosing in our own interests, we often choose unwisely. When employees have the option of participating in a retirement-savings
scheme, many do not, despite the financial advantages of doing
so. If their employer instead automatically enrolls them, giving
them the choice of opting out, participation jumps dramatically.[10] The lesson is that often it doesn't take much of a nudge
to overcome the apathy that gets in the way of our doing what
we know would be best for us. The right kind of nudge—
whether it comes from government, corporations, voluntary
organizations, or even ourselves—can also help us do what we
know we really ought to do.

The investment bank and securities trader Bear Stearns—
before its sale to JPMorgan Chase during the 2008 subprime
mortgage crisis—made sure that neither apathy nor selfishness
prevented its leaders from doing the right thing. One of the
guiding principles listed on its website was a commitment to
philanthropy, based on the belief that a personal commitment
to charity is an underpinning of good citizenship and fosters a
more-rounded individual. This wasn't just window dressing.
Senior managing directors—roughly, the highest-paid thousand employees—were required to give a minimum of 4 percent of their salary and bonus to nonprofit organizations, and
they had to hand in their tax returns to show that they had
done so. The directors gave more than $45 million to charity in
2006. James Cayne, the company's chairman at the time, said
that the rule was part of the company's culture, and that most
people found giving to charity "incredibly gratifying." That

view was echoed by Michele Segalla, then a senior managing director, who found that the policy "gets you to do what you want to do anyways." Segalla also pointed out that people at Bear Stearns talked more about giving than those at another financial firm where she had previously worked. There, it would have been awkward to raise the topic, because you never knew whether your coworkers gave at all. At Bear Stearns, however, directors sent one another memos about their favorite causes, forming a network that made giving more effective.[11]

In an example of how a culture of giving can change, just four days after an article on Bear Stearns's policy of mandatory charitable donations appeared in *The New York Times,* its rival Goldman Sachs announced that it was setting up a new charitable fund called Goldman Sachs Gives, and that the partners had agreed to give a part of their earnings to it. No figure was specified, but Goldman Sachs also announced that it was raising its limit on an annual matching-gift program from $10,000 to $20,000. This program matches charitable gifts made by eligible employees, but not by partners. Many other corporations allow or encourage employees to give time or money to good causes. The supermarket chain Whole Foods Market donates a minimum of 5 percent of its profits to non-profit organizations and gives employees time off with full pay—up to twenty hours a year—to do voluntary community service. Google has set up its own innovative philanthropic arm, Google.org, pledging 1 percent of its profits and equity for ventures that can help the world. Among the projects it supports are clean energy; informing people in developing countries about government services available to them; and finding better ways of predicting droughts before they lead to famines, and of predicting which disease outbreaks may become pandemics. Google's employees may spend 20 percent of their time working with Google.org projects.[12]

If major corporations, universities, and other employers

were to deduct 1 percent of each employee's salary and donate the money to organizations fighting global poverty, *unless* the employee opted out of the scheme, that would nudge employees to be more generous and would yield billions more for combating poverty. It might take some experimentation to find the default level that would yield the greatest sum. If many employees balked at 1 percent, it would be worth trying something less than that. The scale could also be graduated, with a higher default level for higher earners. The important point is to keep the default level below that at which most people would opt out, so that accepting the default level becomes something that almost everyone does. Though the idea may sound odd now, if a few corporations or institutions adopt it, it could spread.

Challenging the Norm of Self-interest

When corporations make giving normal behavior, and when generous people speak openly about how much they give away, they do more than encourage others to do the same. They also challenge an assumption about our behavior that permeates western culture, and particularly American culture: the norm of self-interest.

Alexis de Tocqueville, that sharp observer of the American psyche during the formative years of the United States, noticed the norm even then: "Americans," he wrote in 1835, "enjoy explaining almost every act of their lives on the principle of self-interest." He thought that in doing this they were underplaying their own benevolence, because in his view Americans were, just like everyone else, moved by spontaneous natural impulses to help others. But in contrast to Europeans, he found Americans "hardly prepared to admit that they do give way to emotions of this sort."[13]

Despite the increasing popularity of philanthropy, in some

circles it is still unacceptable to be altruistic, and not only among Americans. Hugh Davidson, who is British, was president of Playtex in Canada and Europe, and has written several successful books on marketing and business management. Although he has set up his own philanthropic foundation, he says: "If you're a philanthropist, you don't tell your friends you're spending your money on charity. You'd sound damn stupid."[14] As this suggests, many of us believe not only that people *are* generally motivated by self-interest, but that they *ought* to be—if not necessarily in the moral sense of "ought" then at least in the sense that they would be foolish, or irrational, if they were not self-interested.

Conversely, when people appear to act contrary to their own interests, we tend to be suspicious, especially if the action is carefully considered (as opposed to something impulsive like jumping onto a subway track to save someone from being hit by an oncoming train). When celebrities like Angelina Jolie or Madonna support organizations that help the poor, we look for hidden selfish reasons. We readily agree with the suggestion that they are doing it only for the publicity. Undeniably selfless behavior makes us uncomfortable. Perhaps that is why we smile tolerantly at the practice of giving away a lot of money in return for naming rights for a concert hall or a wing of an art gallery: It reassures us that the donor is not really selfless, and so does not threaten our assumptions about human motivation.

Several studies have investigated the extent to which we expect that other people will be motivated by self-interest. For example, in one study students were told about a budget proposal to slash research into an illness that affected only women. Asked to estimate what percentage of men and what percentage of women would oppose the proposal, they greatly overestimated the extent to which attitudes were affected by gender. Similarly, they assumed that virtually all smokers would oppose tax increases on cigarettes and restrictions on smoking in public places, and that virtually all nonsmokers would approve of these measures. In reality, people's attitudes were not as closely linked to their interest—or lack of interest—in smoking as the students had expected. As psychologist Dale Miller puts it, on these public policy issues "the small actual effects of self-interest stand in sharp relief to the substantial assumed effects of self-interest." Moreover, the students' own attitudes on the issues were often contrary to their interests—for instance, male participants in the study were likely to oppose the proposal to slash research into the women's illness, while at the same time predicting that most men would support it. This leads Miller to explore a puzzle: "How is it that people come to embrace the theory of self-interest when everyday life provides so little evidence of it?"[15]

Miller began his search for the answer to this question with an experiment conducted by economist Robert Frank. At the beginning and end of a semester, Frank asked his students whether they would return a lost envelope containing $100. Students who took an economics course that semester shifted away from returning the envelope. Students who had taken an astronomy course did not.[16] Perhaps the economics students had gained the impression that everyone is motivated by self-interest. (Economists argue that smokers approve of tax increases on cigarettes because they want to quit and they hope the taxes will make it easier for them to do so.) But you do not need to study economics to be affected by the norm of self-interest. Everyone in a developed society is constantly being bombarded with messages about how to save money, or earn more money, or look better, or gain status—all of which reinforce the assumption that these are things that everyone is pursuing, and that really matter.

The norm of self-interest is so strong that a version of it holds even in nonprofit organizations that rely on the altruism of volunteers. Psychologists Rebecca Ratner and Jennifer Clarke asked volunteers for Students Against Drunk Driving to read applications from two students interested in volunteering for the organization. The applications differed only in that one applicant said that her sister had been killed by a drunk driver, while the other simply said that it is a very important cause. Volunteers were more encouraging and supportive of the applicant whose sister had been killed than they were of the other applicant. Ratner and Clarke suggest that this is because they understand her "self-interested" stake in the cause. They viewed with suspicion the applicant who had a more general altruistic motivation. In this case, as in many others, suspicion of those with apparently altruistic motives seems counterproductive. The organization is unlikely to achieve its objectives if its support is limited to the relatively small number of people who have experienced a personal tragedy at the hands of a drunk driver.[17]

Contrary to what so many of us believe, there is an enormous amount of altruistic, caring behavior in everyday life (even if, for reasons we explored in the previous chapter, not enough of it is directed toward the world's poorest people). However, sociologist Robert Wuthnow found that even people who acted altruistically tended to offer self-interested explanations—sometimes quite implausible ones—for what they had done. They volunteered to work for good causes, they said, because it "gave me something to do," or "got me out of the house." They were reluctant to say: "I wanted to help."

Literature is full of characters like Molière's Tartuffe, who pretend to be altruistically motivated when they are really self-seeking. We have a word for them: hypocrites. But there are fewer examples of people who are really altruistic but pretend to be self-interested, and there is, as far as I know, no single word to describe them. In his book *Acts of Compassion*, Wuthnow offers a striking example of this type. We don't learn how Jack Casey earns an income, but we are told that he does at least fifteen hours a week of volunteer work. He is a member of the local fire department and rescue squad, and teaches first aid and outdoor safety courses to schoolchildren. On one rescue, he swam across an icy lake and saved a woman's life. Yet Casey still says that his own interests come first. On a rescue mission, "I'm number one, my crew is number two, and the patient is number three." When he hears people say that they want to join the rescue squad to help others, Casey says that he knows this isn't the truth: "Deep down, everybody has their own selfish reason; they're really doing it for themselves." Wuthnow traces Casey's attitude to a reluctance to be seen as a "bleeding heart," "goody two-shoes," or "do-gooder." This reluctance, in turn, comes from social norms against being "too charitable" and from our belief that "caring is in some ways deviant, the exception rather than the rule." As Wuthnow points out, however, so many Americans engage in some volunteer work that it isn't deviant in a statistical sense. It is deviant only in terms of the prevailing norm of self-interest.[18]

There is plenty of other evidence all around us that people act from motives other than self-interest. They leave tips when dining at restaurants to which they will never return, sometimes even in towns they don't expect to ever visit again. They donate blood to strangers although that cannot possibly increase their own prospects of getting blood if they should ever need it. They vote in elections when the chance that their vote will tip the balance is vanishingly small. All this suggests that the norm of self-interest is an ideological belief, resistant to refutation by the behavior we encounter in everyday life. Yet we are in thrall to the idea that it is "normal" to be self-interested. Since most of us are keen to fit in with everyone else, we tell stories about our acts of compassion that put a self-interested face on them. As a result, the norm of self-interest appears to be confirmed, and so the behavior continues. The norm is self-reinforcing and yet socially pernicious, because if we believe that no one else acts altruistically, we are less likely to do it ourselves; the norm becomes a self-fulfilling prophecy.

When walking in London, Thomas Hobbes, the seventeenth-century philosopher who famously held that all our actions are self-interested, gave a coin to a beggar. His companion, eager to catch the great man out, told Hobbes that he had just refuted his own theory. Not so, Hobbes responded: He gave the money because it pleased him to see the poor man happy. Hobbes thus avoided the refutation of his theory by widening the notion of self-interest so that it is compatible with a great deal of generosity and compassion. That reminds us that there is both a broad and a narrow sense of self-interest. The long-running debate about whether humans are capable of genuine altruism is, in practical terms, less significant than the question of how we understand our own interests. Will we understand them narrowly, concentrating on acquiring wealth and power for ourselves? Do we think that our interests are best fulfilled by a lifestyle that displays our economic success by our ostentatious consumption of as many expensive items as possible? Or do we include among our interests the satisfactions that come from helping others? Members of the 50% League found that their gifts gave meaning, fulfillment, and even "kicks" to what would otherwise be less-rewarding lives. Does this make their giving self-interested? If so, we need more people who are self-interested like that.

THE FACTS ABOUT AID

6. How Much Does It Cost to Save a Life, and How Can You Tell Which Charities Do It Best?

The argument that we ought to be doing more to save the lives of people living in extreme poverty presupposes that we can do it, and at a moderate cost. But can we? If so, to which organizations should we donate? Holden Karnofsky and Elie Hassenfeld began to tackle these questions a few years ago. It was 2006, they were in their mid-twenties, and the Connecticut hedge fund they worked for was paying them much more than they could reasonably spend. They wanted to donate some of their money to charity but soon found that donating isn't so simple. As successful hedge fund employees, Karnofsky and Hassenfeld wouldn't invest in a company without first getting detailed information on its fundamentals. Now they wanted to make similarly well-informed choices about the charities to which they contributed. With help from six of their friends, they began asking organizations for information that would demonstrate the impact of their work. In return, they received—as one colleague put it—"lots of marketing materials which look nice, you know, pictures of sheep look-ing happy and children looking happy, but otherwise are pretty useless." So they began calling the charities directly and asking detailed questions about what they did with their money and what evidence they had that the money was doing what it was intended to do. It turned out to be surprisingly difficult to get a straight answer. One non-profit representa-tive accused them of trying to steal proprietary information. Another responded that the information they sought was con-fidential.

Finding Charities That Really Make a Difference

You have probably heard questions raised about various chari-ties' use of funds—in particular, about how much of the money they raise actually goes to helping the people it's intended to help, rather than to cover the administrative costs of the home office. The website Charity Navigator focuses attention on this problem by publishing a list of the ten charities that have the highest ratio of administrative expenses to income. As I write, the list is topped by an organization with administrative ex-penses amounting to 77 percent of the money it raises. Unfor-tunately, the exposure of inefficient or downright fraudulent charities often hurts donations to more effective groups. You may well not want to offer your hundred dollars if there's some chance that only twenty-three of them will be used effectively.

Charity Navigator, started in 2001, claims to be America's largest and most widely used evaluator of charities. It pulls to-gether useful information, including the percentages of their income that charities spend on administration. These figures show that the major aid organizations keep their administrative and fund-raising expenses down to around 20 percent of their revenue, and sometimes much less. Yet Charity Navigator's evaluations don't answer Karnofsky and Hassenfeld's key question: How do you know whether the charity is helping the people it's intended to help? One reason the figures don't necessarily tell the full story is that they are taken from forms the charities themselves complete and send to the tax authorities. No one checks the forms, and the breakdown between administrative and program expenses can be massaged with a little creative accounting. For example, staff working in an organization's head office may do some administrative work on an aid program as well as performing more routine office tasks, and in that case their time may be assigned largely to the aid program, so that a high proportion of their salaries is itemized as part of the aid budget, rather than as office expenses. A more significant problem with focusing on how much of its income a charity spends on administration, however, is that this figure tells you nothing at all about the impact the charity is having. Indeed, the pressure to keep administrative expenses low can make an organization less effective. If, for example, an agency working to reduce global poverty cuts staff who have expert knowledge of the countries in which they work, the agency will have lower administrative costs, and may appear to be getting a higher percentage of the funds it receives to people in need. But having removed its experts from the payroll, the agency may well be more likely to end up funding projects that fail. It may not even know which of its projects fail, because evaluating projects, and learning from mistakes, requires highly qualified staff, and paying for them adds to administrative costs.

Karnofsky and Hassenfeld were astonished by how unprepared charities were for questions that went beyond such superficial and potentially misleading indicators of efficacy. Eventually, they realized something that seemed to them quite extraordinary: The reason they were not getting the information they wanted from the charities was that the charities themselves didn't have it. In most cases, neither the charities nor any independent agencies were doing the kind of rigorous evaluation of effectiveness that Karnofsky and Hassenfeld's background in investment management had led them to assume must be the basis of the decisions that major donors made before giving. If the information didn't exist, then both individual donors and major foundations were giving away huge sums with little idea what effect their gifts were having. How could hundreds of billions of dollars be spent without some evidence that the money is doing good?

Having identified the problem, Karnofsky and Hassenfeld decided to do something about it. In 2007 they founded GiveWell, a nonprofit dedicated to improving the transparency and effectiveness of charities. At first they planned to run the organization in their spare time. It soon became clear, however, that the task required full-time attention, so the following year, after raising $300,000 from their fellow workers, they left their hedge fund jobs and began working for GiveWell and its associated grant-making body, the Clear Fund. They invited charities to apply for grants of $25,000 in five broad humanitarian categories, with the application process asking the charities to provide information demonstrating that they were making measurable progress toward achieving their goals, and indicating the cost of their achievements. In this way, the money GiveWell raises is effective in two distinct ways. A substantial part of it—the $25,000 grants—goes to the most effective charity in each category, thus supporting its work. At the same time, the existence of the grants encourages charities to do more to evaluate the effectiveness of what they are doing. Of the five categories, the one most relevant to our concerns was "Saving Lives in Africa." Since Africa has one-third of the world's extremely poor people, with some of the world's highest rates of childhood mortality and shortest overall life expectancy, the information GiveWell seeks is just the information we need to answer the questions posed by the argument set out in this book: Is it true that a relatively modest donation to an aid agency can save a life? And if so, which agencies do this best?

What It Really Costs to Save a Life

For saving lives on a large scale, it is difficult to beat some of the campaigns initiated by the World Health Organization (WHO), an arm of the United Nations founded in 1948 to provide leadership on global health issues. Among its most important accomplishments was its leadership in the fight to end smallpox, which killed between 300 million and 500 million people during the twentieth century.[1] In 1967, the year WHO began a concerted effort to wipe it out, smallpox was still killing 2 million people a year. Twelve years later, it was gone, banished to two highly secure laboratories. WHO has also played a prominent role in the fight against river blindness, a parasitic eye and skin disease that has infected 18 million Africans, of whom roughly 300,000 are blind as a result. To date the program has stopped 600,000 people from going blind, and made it possible to resettle vast tracts of land from which people had fled to avoid the disease. It is hoped that by 2010 treatment will be available to everyone affected and that the disease will cease to be a public health problem. And WHO's immunization campaign against measles in southern Africa helped bring the death toll down from 60,000 children in 1996 to 117 in 2000.[2]

These WHO campaigns have saved lives and prevented blindness. But how efficiently have they used their resources—that is, how much have they cost per life saved? Until we can get closer to answering this question, it's going to be hard to decide how to use our money most effectively. Organizations often put out figures suggesting that lives can be saved for very small amounts of money. WHO, for example, estimates that many of the 3 million people who die annually from diarrhea or its complications can be saved by an extraordinarily simple recipe for oral rehydration therapy: a large pinch of salt and a fistful of sugar dissolved in a jug of clean water. This lifesaving remedy can be assembled for a few cents, if only people know about it.[3] UNICEF estimates that the hundreds of thousands of children who still die of measles each year could be saved by a vaccine costing less than $1 a dose.[4] And Nothing But Nets, an organization conceived by American sportswriter Rick Reilly and supported by the National Basketball Association, provides anti-mosquito bed nets to protect children in Africa from malaria, which kills a million children a year. In its literature, Nothing But Nets mentions that a $10 net can save a life: "If you give $100 to Nothing But Nets, you've saved ten lives."[5]

If we could accept these figures, GiveWell's job wouldn't be so hard. All it would have to do to know which organization can save lives in Africa at the lowest cost would be to pick the lowest figure. But while these low figures are undoubtedly an important part of the charities' efforts to attract donors, they are, unfortunately, not an accurate measure of the true cost of saving a life.

Take bed nets as an example. They will, if used properly, prevent people from being bitten by mosquitoes while they sleep, and therefore will reduce the risk of malaria. But not every net saves a life: Most children who receive a net would have survived without it. Jeffrey Sachs, attempting to measure the effect of nets more accurately, took this into account, and estimated that for every one hundred nets delivered, one child's life will be saved every year (Sachs estimated that on average a net lasts five years). If that is correct, then at $10 per net delivered, $1,000 will save one child a year for five years, so the cost is $200 per life saved (this doesn't consider the prevention of dozens of debilitating but nonfatal cases). But even if we assume that these figures are correct, there is a gap in them—they give us the cost of delivering a bed net, and we know how many bed nets "in use" will save a life, but we don't know how many of the bed nets that are delivered are actually used. And so the $200 figure is not fully reliable, and that makes it hard to measure whether providing bed nets is a better or worse use of our donations than other lifesaving measures.

Karnofsky and Hassenfeld found similar gaps in the information on the effect of immunizing children against measles. Not every child immunized would have come down with the disease, and most who do get it recover, so to find the cost per life saved, we must multiply the cost of the vaccine by the number of children to whom it needs to be given in order to reach a child who would have died without it. And oral rehydration treatment for diarrhea may cost only a few cents, but it costs money to get it to each home and village so that it will be available of when a child needs it, and to educate families in how to use it. One study has indicated that the cost of saving a life by providing education about diarrhea and its treatment can be as little as $14 in areas where the disease is most common, but as much as $500 where diarrhea is less prevalent.[6] Taking all these factors into account, economist William Easterly suggests that the World Health Organization's programs for reducing deaths from malaria, diarrhea, respiratory infections, and measles cost roughly $300 per life saved.[7]

In 2007, GiveWell published the results of its investigation into charities working to save lives and improve health in Africa. The investigation covered only the fifty-nine organizations that applied for a GiveWell grant; of these, only fifteen provided adequate information. The remainder described their activities, offering stories or newspaper articles about particular projects, but no detailed evidence showing the number of people who benefited, and how they benefited, from the organization's activities, and what those activities cost.

GiveWell gave top rating to an organization based in Washington, D.C., called Population Services International (PSI), which sees its mission as harnessing the vitality of the private sector to address the health problems of the poor in developing countries. PSI sells condoms, bed nets, water purification treatment, and treatment for malaria and diarrhea, and educates people on their uses. It sells the items at a nominal cost because evidence suggests that people are more likely to use things properly if they have paid for them. In 2005, PSI sold 8.2 million nets at a cost of $56 million. Using a more conservative estimate than Jeffrey Sachs of the number of children sleeping under each net, and allowing that the nets may be used only 50 to 80 percent of the time, GiveWell gives a range of $623 to $2,367 for the cost per life saved by preventing malaria. PSI's own estimate is $820, a figure that falls between GiveWell's high and low estimates, and that is still more than four times Sachs's estimate.

As for PSI's other major activity, promoting and distributing condoms, GiveWell estimates that each HIV infection averted costs between $200 and $700. (In poor countries where antiretroviral drugs are not available, HIV is a great deal more likely to kill.)

PSI's program to save lives from diarrhea is a relatively minor part of its budget, so GiveWell did not study it as fully as other parts of PSI's operations, but it may be the most cost-effective. PSI distributes products that can be mixed into water to make it safe to drink and to prevent diarrhea. It also distributes oral rehydration treatment. GiveWell's rough estimate is that this program costs $250 per life saved. Since the program plays only a small part in PSI's activities, however, GiveWell estimates that across the organization as a whole, PSI saves lives for between $650 and $1,000 each. In addition, it prevents nonfatal malaria attacks, nonfatal sexually transmitted diseases, unwanted pregnancies, and nonfatal attacks of diarrhea.

GiveWell's other two most effective organizations were Partners in Health and Interplast. We have already come across Partners in Health, cofounded by Paul Farmer and supported by Tom White, a member of the 50% League. From its modest beginnings in Haiti and then Peru, it has now expanded to Rwanda, Lesotho, and Russia, providing free health care to some of the world's poorest people. Although the cost per life saved by its provision of basic health services in impoverished rural areas is relatively high—estimated at $3,500—Partners provides many other health benefits to those it serves.

Interplast doesn't save lives, but GiveWell included it in this category because it transforms them so dramatically. Interplast corrects deformities like cleft palate, and helps burn victims so that they can walk or use their hands again. It organizes surgical team trips, using surgeons and medically trained volunteers from the United States, and it sets up local centers, with training and support, in poor countries. The procedures performed are often relatively simple and would be routine in rich nations, but for the poor in the developing world, getting to a surgeon is often impossible. GiveWell calculates that Interplast spends about $500 to $1,500 per corrective surgery. Life-changing procedures anywhere, the surgeries are even more so in poor countries, where discrimination against people with deformities is often much more severe than in rich nations. According to Interplast, in developing nations only 3 percent of children with disabilities go to school. Finding work is also likely to be much more difficult, and people with severe deformities, especially women, are less likely to be able to marry, which in many societies greatly increases a woman's chance of living in poverty.[8]

Overcoming Poverty

In addition to examining charities that work directly to improve health in Africa, GiveWell undertook a separate investigation of organizations that help the poor improve their income and general standard of living. Here again the major organizations did not provide Karnofsky and Hassenfeld with the information they needed, so they narrowed their focus to one kind of intervention for which some good evidence about benefits exists: microfinance.

The story of microfinance begins in 1976, when Muhammad Yunus was head of the department of economics at Chittagong University in Bangladesh. His research on rural poverty took him to the nearby village of Jobra, where he found that to buy the bamboo they needed, women making furniture had to borrow from local moneylenders who charged such high rates of interest that the women could never work their way out of poverty. Yunus took the equivalent of U.S. $27 from his own pocket and lent it to a group of forty-two women from the village. Incredibly, this tiny sum—about 64 cents per person—was enough to put them on the path to independence from the moneylenders, and to eventually repay the loan and work their way out of poverty.

Encouraged by this success, Yunus persuaded a government bank to lend money for a pilot project that would make very small loans to villagers. Over the next six years, the pilot project made thousands of loans, usually to groups of women. The women knew that if they did not repay the loan, others in the group would not be able to borrow, so virtually all the loans were repaid. This reversed the then-accepted economic wisdom that lending to the poor carries high risks and therefore can only be economically viable if high rates of interest are charged.

In 1982, when it was clear that the concept was working,

Yunus founded the Grameen Bank, or "Village Bank," to provide loans across Bangladesh. Today the Grameen Bank has more than 7 million customers in Bangladesh, and has lent more than $6 billion, with a repayment rate of 97 percent. Most important, Yunus created a model for microcredit, as it has come to be known, that has been followed by thousands of institutions all over the world.

But do the loans really reduce poverty? Go to the website of a microfinance institution and you will find accounts of people who have used tiny loans to build successful businesses. The Grameen Foundation, a charity inspired by Yunus's ideas that operates in twenty-eight countries, tells the story of Marie-Claire, a Rwandan woman who is raising four children alone. With a $40 loan, she was able to start a restaurant and earn enough to pay her children's school fees. And Aurora Matias was making a meager living selling slices of bread and slivers of soap to people in her neighborhood who were too poor to buy a whole loaf of bread or cake of soap. She could have sold more, but did not have the money to buy much stock. A small loan from Opportunity International, another microfinance organization, enabled her to buy in bulk, sell more, and make higher profits. Now her business has grown so much that she employs other workers, and her family has a better home.

Such stories are inspiring, but Karnofsky and Hassenfeld wanted to know how representative they are of people who receive microcredit. They read some research showing that those who get loans generally become better off, but they still needed to be convinced that the loans were responsible for the improvement. It might be the case that people who have enough initiative to get loans would become better off anyway. Then Karnofsky and Hassenfeld read a study in which researchers persuaded a South African microfinance organization to choose at random, and offer loans to, some applicants who had narrowly failed to meet the criteria for receiving a loan. That made it possible to compare those who were randomly chosen to receive loans with others who also narrowly failed to meet the criteria, but were not selected for subsequent approval. The study found that six to twelve months later those who received the loans were 11 percent more likely to be employed, 6 percent less likely to experience severe hunger in their households, and 7 percent less likely to be classified as impoverished. Since the two groups were chosen at random, it appears that the loan made the difference—and, incidentally, making the extra loans turned out to be profitable for the lender.[9]

Even if small loans don't always create successful entrepreneurs, they do help the poor cope with financial emergencies. And sometimes they make it possible for them to eat adequately all year round. When someone falls sick, the family may raise the money to pay for a visit to a doctor by selling a cow or goat, or even part of their land. Small loans make it possible for them to avoid selling their most precious assets and sinking deeper into poverty.

Karnofsky and Hassenfeld concluded that microfinance does help the poor—and the fact that people take out loans, knowing that they will have to repay them, is itself an indication that the microfinance institutions are providing a service that the poor want. Hence, in the absence of equally good information about other means of helping people in poverty increase their income and improve their standard of living, GiveWell awarded Opportunity International its $25,000 grant. GiveWell chose Opportunity International over other microfinance organizations because it was impressed by the 98 percent repayment rate on loans Opportunity International made to groups, and by a specific program the organization operates in Mozambique, where most of its clients are living in extreme poverty.[10]

When GiveWell first invited aid organizations to provide information on their work, the big organizations had little incentive to do so because GiveWell's modest $25,000 grants are hardly worth the staff time involved for organizations with multimillion-dollar budgets. In the long run, though, if Give-Well's model for assessing charities catches on, as it should, a high GiveWell rating will bring a flood of new donations. In turn, other charities will focus on demonstrating their cost-effectiveness so as to improve their GiveWell ratings. Equally important, as people become more confident of the cost-effectiveness of charities, they will become more willing to give.

Proving Effectiveness

Long before Holden Karnofsky and Elie Hassenfeld wondered which organizations would make the best use of their dona-tions, Esther Duflo and Abhijit Banerjee at the Massachusetts Institute of Technology founded the Jameel Poverty Action Lab on the premise that we can and should use scientific methods to find out which aid projects work. As the gold standard of scien-tific rigor they take the random controlled trial used for testing the efficacy of new drugs. In such a trial, half the patients are randomly assigned to receive the new drug, while the other half get a placebo. Randomization ensures that the two groups are not different in any way that could affect the course of their ill-ness or the impact of the drug. We have just seen an example of these methods—the study of the effect of loans given by the South African microfinance organization—which was carried out by associates of the Poverty Action Lab.

Controlled trials have validated Mexico's Programa Nacional de Educación, Salud y Alimentación, known as PROGRESA, a program of incentives for mothers to participate in health edu-cation programs, keep their children in school, and take their children to health clinics for nutritional supplements and a checkup.[11] Positive outcomes from the controlled trials have helped PROGRESA gain more funds for expansion within Mexico, and have led other countries to adopt similar measures. Thanks to controlled trials, we know that providing drugs to kill parasitical worms in Kenyan children improves learning, that education in condom use reduces the likelihood of people getting AIDS, and that offering mothers in India a cheap bag of lentils means that more of them will bring in their children for immunization.[12]

So why don't we test all poverty programs this way? One reason is the cost of administering the trials. Oxfam America found that a random controlled trial of one of its microcredit programs in West Africa would cost almost as much as the project itself. The money would have come out of the budget for the project, with the result that microcredit could be extended to only half as many villages as would otherwise be possible. Oxfam did not go ahead with the randomized trial. This is an understandable decision, but it would probably pay, over the long term, for organizations to set aside some money specifically for proper studies of the effectiveness of their programs. It is better to help only half as many people, but be sure that you are really helping them, than to risk helping no one, especially if a successful project can then be scaled up to reach many more.

On the other hand, some aid projects may bring benefits that cannot be quantified. Oxfam believes in "capacity building"—that is, in assisting the poor to develop their skills to become self-sufficient in various ways, and in assisting communities to create structures that will help people work together to resist oppression and escape poverty. In 2003, I visited one such project in Pune, India. Oxfam Australia was assisting ragpickers, women who make their living by sifting through the town garbage dump to collect not just rags but anything else that can be recycled. When we went to the dump to see them at work, the overpowering stench forced some of our group to retreat to the car, where they stayed with the windows closed for the entire visit. Yet the ragpickers made a remarkable contrast to the filth, for they somehow managed to keep their colorful saris clean and bright while they salvaged metal, glass, plastic, even old plastic bags. They were paid only one rupee—about 3 cents—for a kilogram, or more than two pounds, of plastic. Bad as that sounds, it was an improvement on previous prices, when the ragpickers, who were from the Dalit caste, formerly known as Untouchables, had been isolated and held in contempt as the lowest of the low, exploited economically, and sexually harassed by the dealers to whom they sold their gleanings.

Oxfam had been approached by Laxmi Narayan, a lecturer in adult education at a university in Pune. She had been running a literacy program for ragpickers, but realized that they needed more practical help before they could focus on learning to read and write. With Oxfam's assistance, she helped the women organize themselves into the Registered Association of Ragpickers, which enabled them to demand better prices and protected them from harassment. A big breakthrough came when the association persuaded the Pune Municipal Council to issue ragpickers identity cards that would allow them entry to apartment buildings. Residents were asked to separate their recyclables, and as a result, many ragpickers are now able to work in clean and safe conditions, collecting recyclables directly from homes.

The association began taking on other tasks, like running a savings scheme and a microcredit facility. Interest earned on the pooled savings was used to provide scholarships and school texts for members' children. Previously, small children had worked alongside their mothers in the city dump, but I didn't see any on my visit. I was told that most of the ragpickers now realized that by going to school their children might enjoy opportunities that they had not had themselves.

Before I left Pune, I attended a meeting of the ragpickers,

held in a room in the cramped but tidy district in which they lived. I couldn't understand anything that was said, but the atmosphere was one of wide and lively participation. After the meeting, Narayan told me that the women very much appreciated the support Oxfam had given them, but had said it was time for it to come to an end. The project had achieved its goals, and the Registered Association of Ragpickers was now self-supporting.[13] That surely demonstrates that the project was a success.

Another example of aid that is difficult to evaluate in a randomized manner is Oxfam's work in Mozambique supporting women seeking to improve their legal rights. With a population of 18 million, Mozambique is one of the world's poorest countries, and women are especially at risk of living in extreme poverty. Until 2003, girls in Mozambique could be married as young as fourteen, and because marriage brings money and gifts to the bride's family, many girls from poor families were married very young. The law put married women under their husband's control—for instance, a wife required her husband's consent to take paid work. If a woman's husband died, the couple's home and land belonged to his family. Divorced women had no claim to property, and, like widows, were left penniless and were often reduced to begging. "The old law increased poverty for women," said Maria Orlanda, of the Mozambique Women Lawyers' Association. "They depended on their husbands for assets, and there was no way for them to accumulate wealth of any kind."[14]

In the 1990s, women in Mozambique organized a coalition to end these injustices. Oxfam provided technical support and training in advocacy skills, and assisted organizations from different parts of the country to meet and work together. To help raise public awareness of the need for change, Oxfam also supported a media campaign, involving not only television, radio, and newspapers but also, for the many Mozambicans who do not read and lack access to radio and television, street theater. The campaign won support in many sectors of society and government. In 2003, the national parliament passed a new family law, raising the legal age for marriage to eighteen, allowing women to head families (previously only a man could be the head of a family), and granting women rights over the couple's property after one year of living together in a customary marriage.[15] Oxfam has continued to support the coalition as it tries to educate women about their new rights and to ensure that the law is enforced. Here, too, it isn't possible to quantify the impact of Oxfam's work, but the project appears to have contributed to improving the lives of millions of women living in extreme poverty and without basic rights that we take for granted.

More Good Things That Can Be Done Cheaply

There are many more forms of aid that we can reasonably judge to be highly cost-effective, even without formal studies. Here are a few more examples.

David Morawetz, an Australian, was in his fifties when his father died and left him money that he decided he didn't really need for himself. He set up a foundation and looked around for projects to fund. From Oxfam Australia he learned that for many villages in Tigray, an arid region of Ethiopia, the nearest source of water is more than an hour's walk away. Women and girls have to walk two or three hours a day to fetch water from the nearest river for drinking, cooking, and washing. Animals also use the river, so the water should be boiled to make it safe to drink. But because boiling water consumes scarce fuel, the villagers sometimes drink unsafe water, and some, most often children, die as a result.

While some villages in the region have wells that provide

safe, drinkable water right in the village itself, most cannot afford the equipment necessary to penetrate the hard rock that lies above the water. Morawetz donated $10,000 to bring the drilling equipment to one village of about a thousand people. Now that village has its own well, with a simple hand pump that requires no motor or fuel and is easy to maintain. The women and girls from the village no longer have to spend two to three hours a day fetching water. The women can use the time saved for other activities, and the girls have more time to get an education. When Morawetz visited the village, he was told: "Before we had the well, our children used to die. Now they do not." Managed by a committee of six villagers, three men and three women, the well should supply safe drinking water for a lifetime—at a onetime cost of $10 per user.

Morawetz has also donated to the Nepal branch of Students Partnership Worldwide, an international youth-led charity that specializes in training young people to work on projects that improve the lives of rural people. Most of its volunteers are educated young people from Africa and Asia. Here are some of the projects that Morawetz supported in Nepal.

- Providing arsenic filters to remove high naturally occurring levels of arsenic from drinking water. Cost per family: $3.33.
- Making available cooking stoves that cook a meal in half the time taken using a traditional stove, allowing girls time to go to school. The stoves also use only half as much firewood, saving fuel and reducing greenhouse gas emissions, and have chimneys to remove smoke, thus reducing the incidence of asthma and eye diseases. Cost per family: $20.
- Helping residents of a slum area of Kathmandu build toilets in their homes. Previously, people relieved them-

selves into an open sewer that flowed between their houses. When the toilets were built, the sewer was closed. Cost per home: $22.

In 1989, Magda King led an all-woman expedition to Cho Oyu, at 26,906 feet (8,201 meters) the sixth-highest mountain in the world, situated on the Nepal–Tibet border. She reached the summit herself, thus becoming the first Spanish woman to climb a peak over 8,000 meters. She has since climbed on five continents, and on seven of the fourteen "eight thousanders" in the world. King's climbs have taken her through many remote villages in which people live in poverty. Wanting to give something back to Nepal, and to the Sherpa people who helped her climb, she traveled across the United States, giving talks and slide shows and collecting donations. In a remote area of Nepal, far from the tourist trails, she spent three months working with local people to build a school. Although she told one interviewer, "We build schools at the end of the road," in fact Yarmasing is more isolated than that—it is two hours' hard walking from any road a vehicle can use. On returning home, King and her husband started Namlo International, which focuses on education as a way of helping people in impoverished rural communities escape poverty. (The namlo is the headstrap that makes it possible for Nepalese people to carry heavy loads for long distances.) The entire community must decide that it wants a school and must then cooperate to build it, with outside labor brought in only to do any work that requires skills the villagers do not have. Namlo brings in windows, cement, and other materials, but local stone is used. The work the villagers put in gives them sweat equity, which makes them far more committed to seeing the school succeed, and makes it possible for a school for 200 children to be built for under $25,000.

Completing the actual building is only the first step. Namlo then works with sister schools in the United States to ensure that the schools are properly staffed and provided with books and other teaching materials. Namlo has made a ten-year commitment to support the schools and assist the communities in becoming self-sustaining. For example, Namlo gave financial support to four village women so they could go to Kathmandu to learn a traditional method of weaving. The women will return to the village and teach other women, providing them with a source of income. Namlo also helps with adult literacy programs and with community infrastructure, like providing a safe water supply.

King says her mountaineering expeditions were "about me, but also for women in Spain, to show that we were capable of doing such things." Nevertheless, she says, her work with the rural communities Namlo serves has enriched her life more than anything else she has done. Through it, "I have reached goals that are much higher than standing on top of the highest mountain in the world." She also believes that she has shown that we are not powerless to bring about change: One person can make a difference to entire communities.

Australian ophthalmologist Fred Hollows traveled to Nepal and Eritrea in the 1980s and was struck by the number of people blinded by cataracts and other treatable eye problems. From then until his death in 1993, he worked tirelessly to bring simple sight-restoring procedures to people who would otherwise have no access to them. A year before he died, knowing that he had cancer and not much time left, Hollows and his wife, Gabi, set up the Fred Hollows Foundation to carry on his work. By 2003 the foundation had restored sight to a million people, at a cost of roughly $50 per person.[16]

It's easy to appreciate that being blind in a poor country, where there is little support for people with disabilities, is significantly worse than being blind in a rich nation. Restoring sight not only greatly helps the individual person, it also enables him or her to contribute once again to his or her family or community. In India, according to one study, 85 percent of men and 58 percent of women who lost their jobs because of blindness were able to regain employment after their sight had been restored. In the case of children, preventing or overcoming blindness can be lifesaving; studies show that children who become blind are much more likely to die within the next year than other children. Those who survive are unlikely to be able to attend school.

Another example of how a relatively small amount of money (for most people living in rich nations) can make a totally life-changing difference to someone who is poor comes from the treatment of obstetric fistulas. In cultures where girls are poorly nourished or are married before their bodies properly mature, they often become pregnant before the pelvis is large enough for the delivery of the baby. As a result, the baby becomes stuck during labor; birth may be obstructed for several days. For a woman giving birth in a village without modern medical techniques, this almost always means that the baby dies. Meanwhile, the pressure of the baby's head against the wall of the vagina can produce a hole, or fistula, between the vagina and either the bladder or the rectum. Urine or feces will then trickle through the vagina. No matter how much she washes, the woman will give off a foul smell. The husband, who may believe his wife has been cursed, often returns her to her family. The family, unable to cope with her inside the home, builds a small hut for her. There she will live alone for the rest of her life.

In 1959, Catherine and Reginald Hamlin, specialists in obstetrics and gynecology from Australia and New Zealand, visited Ethiopia, and after seeing the problems women there faced due to the lack of medical care, decided to stay. Discovering that general hospitals often turn away women with fistulas, because their condition is not life-threatening and they are difficult to keep clean, the Hamlins established the Addis Ababa Fistula Hospital. Bringing fistula patients together had the additional advantage, they discovered, that women who had been isolated for years were now able to have a social life and to talk to others with the same problem. Since her husband's death, Catherine Hamlin has continued to work in Ethiopia for fistula patients, and the hospital has now treated 32,000 women and trained both medical students and surgeons. Support from the Fistula Foundation, a California-based charity, has made it possible to open three mini-hospitals in other parts of Ethiopia. Now in her eighties, Hamlin has appeared on *Oprah* and in an inspiring *Nova* documentary, *A Walk to Beautiful.* The hospital never turns away a woman with a fistula, and is able to cure 93 percent of its patients. When they are ready to go, the women are given their bus fare home and a new dress. Here Hamlin describes a scene she has seen thousands of times: "We've got this girl with her whole life ahead of her, and if she's not cured it's going to be a misery and a horror to her forever. So the joy of seeing a young girl normal again and going home in a new dress with a smile on her face and literally on dancing feet is something that really warms our hearts."[17]

According to a report by the United Nations Population Fund and EngenderHealth, an American women's health organization, the cost of repairing a standard fistula in Africa is between $100 and $400.[18] The Worldwide Fistula Fund, another charity supporting fistula care, puts the cost of surgical care for a single fistula victim at $450.[19]

When I met Lewis Wall, founder, president, and managing director of the Worldwide Fistula Fund, at Washington University in St. Louis, where he also serves as professor of obstetrics and gynecology, he was about to leave for Niger. His fund is building a new specialist fistula hospital in an area with a particularly high rate of obstetric fistulas. Wall told me there are 3 million women living with untreated fistulas, with at least

33,000 more acquiring the condition in Africa alone each year.[20] In Liberia the previous summer, he had operated on a sixty-seven-year-old who had developed a fistula when she was thirty-two and had been living soaked with urine for thirty-five years. "It took twenty minutes to repair it in surgery," he told me. The only long-term solution is prevention, especially increasing awareness of the risks to girls of bearing children too young. Better access to emergency obstetric centers would also dramatically reduce the problem. But in the meantime, he asks, "What is it worth to give a fourteen-year-old girl back her future and her life?"

. . .

It's difficult to calculate how much it costs to save or transform the life of someone who is extremely poor. We need to put more resources into evaluating the effectiveness of various programs. Nevertheless, we have seen that much of the work done by charities is highly cost-effective, and we can reasonably believe that the cost of saving a life through one of these charities is somewhere between $200 and $2,000.

Even at the upper end of this range, the contrast between what it costs to save a life in a poor nation and how much we spend to save lives in rich nations should make us uncomfortable. A 1995 Duke University study of more than five hundred lifesaving interventions in the United States put the median cost of saving a life at $2.2 million.[21] In 2008, the U.S. Environmental Protection Agency valued a generic American life at $7.22 million, while the federal Department of Transportation uses a figure of $5.8 million.[22] (Government agencies use these figures to judge whether measures that save lives by, for example, reducing air pollution or building safer roads are economically justifiable.)

Amid such uncertainty, what should we do? There are many organizations doing good work that offer opportunities worth supporting, and not knowing which is the very best shouldn't be an excuse for not giving to any of them. If you have a spare $450 and are thinking about whether to spend it on yourself or to use it to help others, it won't be easy to find anything that you need nearly as much as a fourteen-year-old girl with a fistula needs an operation. If you have only $50, you can make the same comparison between what the money means to you and what it could mean to someone who is unable to see because of an easily removable cataract.

7. Improving Aid

Though we have already looked briefly at some common objections to aid, we haven't yet done justice to the serious critics who point out that many aid programs have failed to reduce poverty. Prominent among these critics is economist William Easterly, who laments the ineffectiveness of aid:

> The West spent $2.3 trillion on foreign aid over the last five decades and still had not managed to get twelve-cent medicines to children to prevent half of all malaria deaths. The West spent $2.3 trillion and still had not managed to get four-dollar bed nets to poor families. . . . It's a tragedy that so much well-meaning compassion did not bring these results for needy people.[1]

Did you get the impression that the West has already shown great compassion and given enormous sums of foreign aid? We have already seen that most western nations are giving very little aid, as a proportion of their national income. But Easterly is talking about the past five decades, so before we get to the issue of aid's effectiveness, let's first do some Q&A on how much aid the West has really given during this period.

Q: How much per year is $2.3 trillion over five decades?

A: $46 billion.

Q: How much per person living in affluent nations during that period is $46 billion?

A: There are roughly a billion people living in affluent nations now, but the average over the fifty-year period is around 750 million people. That works out to about $60 per person per year.

Q: What percentage of the total income of the affluent nations over that period is $46 billion?

A: Aid over that period was about 0.3 percent or 30 cents of every $100 earned.[2]

Now the amount of aid that the rich nations are giving doesn't seem so large, does it?

Even the figure of 30 cents given in aid from every $100 earned seriously exaggerates the amount that the rich nations are giving to help the world's poorest people. Much of our aid is based on political or defense priorities rather than humanitarian considerations. During the Cold War, for example, aid from the West was heavily tilted toward luring Third World countries away from Soviet influence. The hundreds of millions of dollars that went into the Swiss bank accounts of the Congolese dictator Mobutu Sese Seko are part of the "aid" that is included in Easterly's figure. No surprise that it did little to reduce poverty.

Although the Cold War is over, statistics available on the website of the Organisation for Economic Co-operation and Development show that aid is still not given solely—or in some cases, even primarily—to relieve global poverty. Consider the top ten recipients of U.S. official development aid. At the time of this writing (June 2008) they are, in order, Iraq, Afghanistan, Sudan, Colombia, Egypt, Ethiopia, the Democratic Republic of Congo, Nigeria, Pakistan, and Jordan. Iraq alone received 29.5 percent of the U.S. foreign aid budget in 2007, and Afghanistan received nearly 6 percent. In contrast, the ten poorest countries in the world receive a combined total of 5 percent of U.S. aid.[3]* Iraq, Afghanistan, and Pakistan are among the U.S. top ten because of their central role in the war on terror, rather than because of their poverty. Egypt has ranked near the top for decades, because it is an important partner in U.S. efforts to stabilize the Middle East, and aid to Jordan has the same motivation. Colombia is not an especially poor country; its aid is associated with the attempt to suppress the cocaine cartels. Only about one fifth of U.S. aid goes to countries classified by the OECD as "least developed," while about half of all U.S. aid goes to "lower-middle-income" nations.

Nor is it only the United States that gives aid to serve political aims rather than to help the extremely poor. Branko Milanovic, an economist at the World Bank, has examined the 2001 country-to-country aid disbursed by most OECD countries, and found that bilateral aid from the European Union—that is, the program run by the EU itself, which is separate from the individual aid programs of its member nations—is even more skewed than U.S. aid toward nations with a per capita income above the world average. Bilateral aid from Australia and Canada in that year was also pro-rich in the sense that richer countries received more money in per capita terms than did poorer countries. Bilateral aid from Germany, France, and Italy was roughly evenly balanced in per capita terms be-

---

*The ten poorest countries are: Central African Republic, Sierra Leone, Eritrea, Niger, Malawi, Ethiopia, Liberia, Guinea-Bissau, Burundi, and the Democratic Republic of Congo.

tween the richer and poorer countries, while aid from Belgium, Ireland, Britain, Switzerland, Luxembourg, the Netherlands, and the Scandinavian nations was strongly tilted toward the poorer countries. Overall, though, only about a quarter of the aid from OECD donor countries goes to the world's least developed countries.[4]

A second reason that total figures for aid can give an exaggerated impression of what is being done to help the poor is that some countries, including the United States and Australia, tie their aid to the purchase of goods that they make, thus boosting their own economies but making the aid less effective. For example, the U.S. Congress requires that U.S. government agencies donating condoms intended to stop the spread of AIDS in Africa must buy the condoms from U.S. manufacturers, although U.S.-made condoms are twice the price of similar products made in Asia. Donating condoms to Africa saves lives, but since the amount of money available for this purpose is fixed, anything that increases the cost of the condoms reduces the number donated and costs lives.[5] A much greater problem, however, is that the roughly $2 billion worth of U.S. aid that consists of food must, by law, be grown in the United States and shipped, mostly on American ships, to wherever it is needed. This helps American farmers sell their crops at good prices, and is also a boon for American shipping companies, but it would be far cheaper to buy the grain in the region where it is needed, saving on shipping costs and other overheads, as well as avoiding a delay of about four months in delivery of the food. Worse still, in terms of effectiveness, importing large quantities of subsidized food depresses local markets, reducing the incentive for farmers in developing countries to become more productive. As Peter Matlon, a director of the Rockefeller Foundation and an agricultural economist, has put it, this is a case of "the tail wagging the dog," in that domestic farm policies have shaped the methods that the United States uses to fight hunger abroad. The U.S. Government Accountability

Office, the nonpartisan investigative arm of Congress, has concluded that food aid is "inherently inefficient," while Daniel Maxwell and Christopher Barrett, in their major study *Food Aid After Fifty Years,* dispel what they refer to as the "myth" that American food aid is primarily about feeding the hungry. These disadvantages have become sufficiently clear for CARE, one of the largest agencies working against poverty, to refuse to distribute American grain in poor countries, even though it would have received $45 million if it had been prepared to do so.[6]

Now, one can make the argument that it's entirely reasonable for countries to make their aid conditional in this way, but if you do, it isn't fair to conclude that all aid is ineffective. Part of the aim of tied aid is to benefit the donor nation's own economy, and presumably it sometimes does achieve this. If we take into account the factors mentioned above, we find that what was actually spent over the past five decades on aid intended primarily to benefit people living in extreme poverty was nothing like $60 per year for each citizen of the wealthy nations. It may have been less than a quarter of that amount. Suppose, though, that the full $60 had gone to aid for the poorest. That's still less than you may spend, without much thought at all, on an evening out. It's less than the price of a ticket to a rock concert, or less than the cost of dinner, a movie, a drink or two, and cab fare or parking. Does the cost of one night out really amount to what Easterly calls "so much well-meaning compassion"? That suggests low expectations of the compassion of our fellow human beings. It also means that we cannot sweepingly condemn aid as ineffective by claiming that our immense compassion has already led us to pour vast sums of aid into poor nations, but that these vast sums have failed to do even basic things like prevent malaria deaths. If we haven't yet succeeded in doing these basic things, maybe it is because what we have given specifically for them was too little.

Most aid critics target government-run programs and

government-funded institutions. Easterly's book *The White Man's Burden,* for example, focuses mainly on the World Bank, the International Monetary Fund, the United Nations, and the United States Agency for International Development (USAID). Easterly argues that these organizations' failures result from grandiose ambitions, top-down planning, and a lack of accountability. But he almost entirely ignores the work of nongovernmental organizations: They are mentioned only four times in a book of four hundred pages, and in none of these references is there a sustained discussion of the NGOs' work. Major individual aid organizations, for example CARE, Oxfam, Save the Children, and World Vision, do not appear at all. Thus, while Easterly advises activists to "change your issue from raising more aid money to making sure that the aid money reaches the poor," he supplies no basis for his suggestion that raising more aid money is futile, if the activist addressed is raising money for a nongovernmental organization. (I have yet to be approached by a fund-raiser asking me to donate to the World Bank.)

Because it hasn't been tried, no one really knows whether poverty on a global scale can be overcome by a truly substantial amount of aid provided without political interference. The political and bureaucratic constraints that encumber official aid only make private donations to effective nongovernmental agencies all the more important. As Easterly himself says, the annual total amount of foreign aid for the world's approximately 3 billion poor people (this figure includes those who are living on less than $2 per day, as well as those who are living on less than $1.25 per day) comes to only about $20 per person. Should we be surprised that this paltry sum hasn't ended poverty? The worst that can be said with any certainty is that in the past, a lot of official aid has been misconceived and misdirected and has done little good. But it scarcely seems possible that, if we truly set out to reduce poverty, and put resources into doing so that match the size of the problem—including resources to evaluate past failures and learn from our mistakes— we will be unable to find ways of making a positive impact.

"Trade, Not Aid"?

One of our great anxieties about giving aid is that it isn't really going to help the poor or, worse still, that it may even hurt them. That view is supported by some aid critics, who claim that aid does not spur economic growth.[7] Martin Wolf, for example, in *Why Globalization Works,* argues that reducing the barriers that poor nations face when they seek to sell their products on the global market would do more to reduce poverty than any amount of aid.[8] Wolf and other aid critics point out that the nations that have pulled themselves out of poverty during the past fifty years have generally received little aid, whereas the nations that have received the most aid are generally still poor. In some cases, this could be because more aid goes to those countries facing greater problems, whether they stem from geographical disadvantages, corruption, customs that inhibit productivity, or poor public policies that reduce the incentives for people to start new businesses. But it's clear that some aid initiatives *have* failed to promote economic growth. It's important to know what the problems are, but also to understand that the right kind of aid can help the poor whether or not it promotes economic growth.

One reason that aid could slow economic growth is "Dutch disease," a term *The Economist* coined to describe a decline in the Dutch economy in the 1960s after natural gas was discovered in the North Sea on the country's coast. This valuable natural resource should have been a great economic boon, but in fact, as the revenues from gas exports began flowing in, Dutch manufacturing slumped. The reason, according to economists, was that as other countries bought Dutch oil, sending money into the country, the value of Dutch currency rose relative to that of the country's main trading partners, thus making Dutch exports more expensive and Dutch manufacturers less competitive in international markets. The inflow of a large amount of foreign aid can cause a similar problem.

Although, as we have seen, aid is a tiny percentage of the income of affluent donor nations, the poor nations are so poor that in some cases aid amounts to more than 10 percent of their national income. In a handful of very poor countries, such as the Democratic Republic of Congo, East Timor, and Afghanistan, aid amounts to more than a quarter of the national income.[9] At that level, aid can cause a very substantial Dutch disease effect. And indeed, economists Raghuram Rajan and Arvind Subramanian have found that aid does significantly reduce the growth of labor-intensive manufacturing industries and export industries, such as food processing and the production of clothing and footwear, in developing countries. Encouragingly, though, in the most recent decade they studied—the 1990s—aid had a slightly less-adverse impact than in the previous decade, perhaps because governments of poor countries were making better use of the aid they received.[10]

Rajan and Subramanian leave it open whether the effects they observed were sufficiently large to offset the benefits of aid. When aid is used to improve infrastructure, agricultural methods, and the skill levels of the workforce, it enhances productivity and leads to increased exports that can outweigh the Dutch disease problem. For ten years after the end of Mozambique's civil war in 1992, European nations gave an extraordinarily high level of aid to that African country; in fact, over those years, 40 percent of the nation's gross national income was foreign aid. Although almost half of the aid was debt relief, which therefore could not be spent within Mozambique, aid was used to build roads, hospitals, and schools and to improve workforce skills.[11] Perhaps for this reason, real economic growth per capita was also high, averaging 5.5 percent per annum. High levels of aid to Botswana after independence in 1966, to Taiwan in the 1950s, and to Uganda in the 1990s also proved compatible with strong economic growth. These examples prove that Dutch disease is by no means inevitable.[12]

In any case, when it comes to barriers to the growth of export industries in developing countries, there is something much more significant than aid-related Dutch disease. U.S. and European agricultural subsidies undercut poor countries' efforts to increase their exports in an economic sector where their climate and cheap labor give them a natural competitive advantage. Take, as an example, cotton, the only source of income for millions of peasant farmers in West Africa, many of whom are supporting families on less than $1.25 a day. They produce cotton more cheaply, and in a more ecologically sustainable way, than the 25,000 highly mechanized and much wealthier cotton growers in the United States. But the United States pays a total of $3 billion a year in subsidies to its cotton growers, enabling them to undercut the West African cotton growers on the world market. Daniel Sumner, who directs the University of California Agricultural Issues Center, has calculated that if the United States were to end its cotton subsidy, the resulting rise in the income of a West African cotton grower would be enough to cover all health care costs for four children.[13] The elimination of all agricultural subsidies and a 50 percent reduction in nonagricultural tariffs would, according to a study by economists Kym Anderson and Alan Winters, mean a global economic gain of at least $96 billion annually, of which $30 billion would go to the developing world.[14] The elimination of subsidies on cotton, corn, and other farm products, which cost taxpayers in the United States and Europe billions, should be a priority on both humanitarian and basic economic grounds.

You might now ask whether it would be better to spend our time and money campaigning to eliminate trade barriers, rather than donating to agencies that give aid to the poor. Obviously this depends on a variety of factors: whether our money and time would make the success of such a campaign more likely, how great the gain for the poor would be if such a campaign succeeded, and how much good our donation could do if given for other forms of aid. The powerful political interests allied against the elimination of trade barriers make political change unlikely. We saw that clearly in the battle over America's 2008 Farm Bill, which authorizes the country's agricultural subsidies. The bill was opposed not only by organizations fighting global poverty, but by virtually every economist in the country other than those working for the farm lobby. President George W. Bush himself called the bill, which provides for $300 billion of subsidies over five years, "bloated and wasteful" and vetoed it. But Congress easily mustered the two-thirds majority required to overturn the veto.[15] Defeats like this suggest that our efforts are better spent elsewhere, where we can be confident of making a difference.

It's important to note, too, that economic growth can bypass people, regions, and even entire nations. That may be because a developing country's government is following ill-advised economic policies or because politics, customs, and social structures are so inimical to economic productivity that few are willing to invest (in which case economic aid can be made conditional on policy reform), but it may also be because the nation suffers from geographical disadvantages—being landlocked, say, and surrounded by poor neighbors that do not offer promising markets. Then growth may be blocked by the difficulty of reaching more prosperous markets for the nation's exports. In those situations, aid aimed at improving local food production and providing education and basic health care may be the best, indeed the only, way of helping the nation's poor.

Ideally, aid should provide a safety net for those who for whatever reason are not benefiting from economic growth. Sometimes poorer countries do better on key indicators of human well-being, such as infant mortality and longevity, than richer ones. Cuba, famously, has lower infant mortality than the United States.[16]

When Easterly and Bill Gates were on a panel together at the World Economic Forum in 2007, Easterly made his usual point that all the aid given to Africa over the years has failed to stimulate economic growth there. Gates responded sharply: "I don't promise that when a kid lives it will cause a GNP increase. I think life has value."[17] Gates is right. Our focus should not be growth for its own sake, but the goals that lie behind our desire for growth: saving lives, reducing misery, and meeting people's basic needs.

Bad Institutions Undo Good Projects

In the long-running debate about why some nations are rich and others are poor, many experts emphasize the importance of good institutions and practices, like the rule of law, protection of property rights, effective government, social conventions that make trust possible, good and universal schooling, and low tolerance of corruption. Effective government means that the public sector works tolerably well. If we want to start a business, we won't have to bribe officials to get things done, and our rights as workers, consumers, and residents will be protected from unsafe workplaces, unsafe products, and industrial pollution. The rule of law protects us from violence and allows us to plan for the future with reasonable confidence that what we own will not be taken from us. It enables us to make contracts, knowing that the other contracting parties will be penalized if they breach them. Since there are always costs in resorting to the law, however, a certain level of trust makes it easier for people to work together and creates a sense of community.

The idea that good institutions play a crucial role in reducing poverty leads not to denying the value of aid, but rather to making aid conditional on the recipient government's doing its part in providing the conditions for economic growth. This way of thinking persuaded President Bush to set up, with bipartisan support, the Millennium Challenge Account, an initiative reserving a portion of U.S. aid for governments that, in the president's words, "govern justly, invest in their people and encourage economic freedom."[18] Organizations like Oxfam have turned their attention to institution-building, supporting the formation of local, democratically run cooperatives to facilitate everything from maintaining a well to marketing coffee, while the World Bank and government-to-government aid programs have sought to build the capacities of governments to function effectively.

And indeed, aid can be effective in improving institutions, as economist Paul Collier has demonstrated, particularly when dealing with fragile states. Nations emerging from civil war, for instance, are at high risk of falling back into conflict, with all the misery that that will bring to their citizens. Collier showed that substantial amounts of aid, properly directed and sustained for several years, can enhance the capacity of postconflict governments to avoid that tragedy.[19] Mozambique, which suffered through decades of internal war, is one example where aid has made a difference. Sierra Leone is proving to be another, although there the danger of a resumption of fighting has not completely passed. Opportunities arise, too, when a reforming government replaces a corrupt or incompetent one, as in the case of Levy Mwanawasa's government in Zambia, which replaced an extremely corrupt government when it took office in 2002. Collier found that in such cases providing $1 billion of technical assistance over four years could be expected to produce $15 billion worth of economic benefits to the nation, not counting the gain to the world that comes from having the country governed effectively.[20]

If we can improve institutions we should do so; in the circumstances Collier describes, it should be our first priority. Tragically, sometimes conditions may be so bad that nothing we can do will diminish the misery of the unfortunate citizens. Then we have to go elsewhere. But at other times aid can directly help the poorest, making a significant and sustainable difference to them, even if it does not lead to better institutions. In that case, we should not withhold it.

The Millennium Villages Project

Right now, a large-scale experiment is taking place in Africa that will test the difference aid can make to rural villagers even without changing their country's larger institutions. Economist Jeffrey Sachs believes that poverty can be a self-reinforcing trap. Small farmers growing cereals in Africa have to contend with poor soils, but cannot afford fertilizer. They save the seeds from the crops they grow, but these are low-yielding varieties. Therefore they get only about a third of the average yield of farmers in developing countries outside Africa, not enough to provide them with the cash to buy fertilizer or better seeds. When the then-UN secretary general Kofi Annan appointed Sachs director of the UN Millennium Villages Project, in 2002, Sachs set out to identify practical and reliable ways of helping the poor escape the poverty trap. He concluded that if for a few years an aid agency provided rural farmers with the means to buy the fertilizers and better seeds they need, they would be able to reinvest what they earned from their improved yields. Even after the agency ceased its support, they would continue to enjoy higher productivity and could invest in further improvements. As Sachs writes: "Temporary assistance can put the farmers on the path of long-term growth. It's not a hunch. Asia's Green Revolution worked that way."[21]

In 2005, Sachs began putting this theory into practice. He came up with a three-way alliance comprising the United Nations Development Programme; Millennium Promise, an NGO; and the Earth Institute at Columbia University, which provides the research and expertise to solve problems in agriculture, public health, engineering, and ecology. Together they are supporting the Millennium Villages Project. Whereas many aid programs are set up to do just one thing—distribute better seeds to improve crop yields, set up schools, or establish health clinics—the Millennium Villages Project aims to do it all at once, offering rural communities multipronged assistance in dealing with a variety of the problems they face.[22]

The project began with twelve villages, with a total of 60,000 inhabitants, all located in chronic hunger "hot spots" that combine serious disease problems with poor health care and infrastructure. All of the villages are in countries that are reasonably peaceful and that, despite varying degrees of corruption, are governed effectively enough for people to farm their land in reasonable security and to retain the profits from any surplus they sell. To test his model under different circumstances, Sachs selected the villages from ten African countries with a variety of climates and agricultural traditions. Although national governments give small amounts of money or services to support the program, all aid is channeled directly to the villages.

The Millennium Villages Project allows each community to choose, in discussion with advisers from the project, the form of assistance it believes will be most desirable and cost-effective for its specific circumstances. The village can choose among programs that provide safe drinking water, vitamin and mineral supplements for children, immunization programs, bed nets, and a deworming program to get rid of internal parasites. As a condition of the grants, women must be allowed to participate in the decisions. The program also offers farmers fertilizer and better varieties of seeds to improve returns in agriculture, as well as advice on diversification into cash crops. The farmers are in turn asked to give a portion of their increased harvest to a program that feeds children at school. This nourishes the children, improves school attendance, and ensures that students are better able to concentrate on their lessons. The program introduces new technologies such as energy-saving stoves, local forms of energy production, and even mobile phones. All in all, the aid costs about $110 per person per year, of which $10 per person must come from the village; the project commits to continuing the aid for five years. After that period, if the plan works, improved yields will allow the farmers to escape the poverty trap, and be able to buy their own fertilizer and become self-sustaining, or diversify into other enterprises. Outside assistance can then be withdrawn.[23]

As of 2008, the program had been extended to eighty villages comprising more than 400,000 people. Initial indications are that crop yields are up substantially, hunger is being eliminated, malnutrition and malaria are declining, and school attendance is sharply rising. Perhaps most important of all, local leaders speak of a new spirit of hope and self-respect among the villagers because they are working together to tackle common problems.

The community leaders from the various villages tell stories of progress. Elizabeth Appiah, the community leader from the village of Bonsaaso in Ghana, wrote of how the project has increased the involvement of women in community work, in part by repairing wells that, back in use, save them two hours of walking per day to fetch water, but also by giving them new opportunities to earn income and participate in a new community learning center. Pamela Mito, the community leader of Sauri, Kenya, says that crop yields have tripled, and that farmers have learned to diversify their agricultural production, so they can now feed themselves and also earn some cash income. She also no longer has to worry about her children getting diarrhea, because the village water supply has been made safe. Yacouba Coulibaly, from Tiby, Mali, says that crop yields have increased enough to give them a surplus to sell, while new separate toilets at the school mean that girls now also attend. For Ndahayo Celestin, of Mayange, Rwanda, the higher yields enable his family to eat two meals a day rather than the one they ate for the previous two years. They are even accumulating cash reserves "so that the future will not be like the past."

So far, then, the indications are good, but it is still too early to tell whether the experiment has vindicated Sachs's "poverty trap" theory and shown that it is possible to end hunger, reduce childhood mortality, and help Africans create a better life for themselves, without building better institutions at a national level. Sometime around 2010–2012 it should become clear whether the Millennium Villages Project is succeeding. If it is, it can be scaled up to reach hundreds of thousands of villages in the many poor countries that have institutions adequate to allow the villages to reap the benefits of higher crop yields, safe water, better health, new schools, and improved communications. That will require more aid, but the aid will prove its effectiveness when the villages that receive assistance become self-sustaining.

The Planet Can't Hold Them

When speaking to audiences about global poverty, I'm often challenged along the following lines: "Saving the lives of poor people now will only mean that more will die when the population eventually crashes because our planet has long passed its carrying capacity." The challenge is evidence of the continuing relevance of the thought of the eighteenth-century English economist and clergyman Thomas Malthus, who famously claimed that population would always outstrip food supplies. If epidemics and plagues did not keep human population in check, he wrote, then "gigantic inevitable famine" would do so.[24] Two centuries later, in 1968, entomologist Paul Ehrlich warned in his bestseller *The Population Bomb* that we had lost the battle to feed humanity. He predicted that by 1985 the world would be swept by "vast famines" in which "hundreds of millions of people are going to starve to death."[25] Fortunately, he was wrong. Food production grew strongly, on a per capita basis, in the three decades after he made his dire prediction, and the proportion of people living in developing countries who were not getting 2,200 calories per day—a basic sufficiency—declined from more than one in two to just one in ten.[26]

In 2008, we again saw headlines about a world food crisis, as wheat hit its highest price in twenty-eight years, the price of corn was double what it had been two years earlier, and the food bill of developing countries rose 25 percent in a year. In the United States, even the poorest fifth of the population spends only 16 percent of its income on food, but in Nigeria the figure is 73 percent, in Vietnam 65 percent, and in Indonesia 50 percent, so higher prices obviously make it harder for the poor to buy enough food to survive.[27] Such developments tend to lead to a revival of Malthusian objections to helping the poor survive and reproduce. But the problem is not that we are producing too little food; rather, we're not eating the food we grow. One hundred million tons of corn is annually turned into biofuel that goes into American gas tanks. That's a lot less corn available for export, and so it contributes to higher world grain prices. But most corn isn't eaten by humans; it's eaten by animals, and that's where the biggest part of the food crisis starts. The amount of grains and soybeans fed to animals has increased sharply over the past decade as Asian nations have become more prosperous, and their citizens have started eating more meat. In China alone, in the two decades up to 2006, the number of beef cattle produced annually increased from fewer than 5 million to more than 50 million, laying hens from 655 million to 2.3 billion, ducks from 300 million to 2 billion, and chickens from 1.5 billion to 7.7 billion. Virtually all of these animals are fed grain and soybeans.[28] According to the United Nations Food and Agriculture Organization, 756 million tons of grain were fed to animals in 2007.[29] Just to give you a sense of how much grain that is, imagine it equally divided among the 1.4 billion people living in extreme poverty. It would give each of them more than half a ton of grain, or about 3 pounds per day, which gives you twice as many calories as you need. Add to that most of the world's 225-million-ton soybean crop, which is also fed to animals, and you can see how much of the food we grow is not eaten directly by humans. When we use animals to convert crops into meat, eggs, or milk, the animals use most of the food value to keep warm and develop bones and other parts we can't eat. Most of the food value of the crops we have grown is wasted—in the case of cattle, we get back only 1 pound of beef for every 13 pounds of grain we feed them. With pigs the ratio is 6 pounds of grain to 1 pound of pork. And even these figures underestimate the waste, because meat has a higher water content than grain.[30] The world is not running out of food. The problem is that we—the relatively affluent—have found a way to consume four or five times as much food as would be possible, if we were to eat the crops we grow directly.

The difference between the present situation and the one Malthus predicted is that while he envisaged the growth of population leading to mass famines, so far the only looming "danger" is mass vegetarianism. The grain and soy we feed to animals gives us a handy buffer against starvation, should we need it. We do produce enough to feed everyone on the planet, and even enough for the additional 3 billion people we can expect to be sharing it with by 2050.

Nevertheless, the world cannot support an indefinitely growing population; in some countries, population growth is already undermining gains in food production. By 2050 Nigeria, now with 144 million people, is expected to grow to 282 million and be the world's sixth most populous nation. By then the Democratic Republic of the Congo, now home to 63 million people, is predicted to have 187 million, and Ethiopia, 77 million today, is expected to have a population of 146 million.[31] But to say, as ecologist Garrett Hardin did in the 1970s with countries like Bangladesh and India in mind, that we should not give aid to poor countries with rapidly growing populations ignores the well-established fact that reducing poverty also reduces fertility.[32] Where many children die and there is no Social Security, parents tend to have large families to ensure that some will survive to look after them in their old age, and, in the case of rural families, to work the land. As countries industrialize and living standards rise, fertility rates fall. This happened in Europe and North America, and then also in those Asian nations that have achieved similar levels of affluence, including Japan and most recently, Korea.

Education also reduces fertility, particularly when offered to girls. In Ethiopia, women who did not go to school have an average of six children; if most of them survive, this would lead to unsustainable population growth. Women who have at least a secondary education have, on average, two children, which is below the replacement level. In other countries the difference is not quite as pronounced, but overall, women with a secondary education give birth to between one-third and one-half as many children as women with no formal education.[33] Reflecting this difference is the Indian state of Kerala. Although it is one of the poorer parts of the country, it has higher literacy and greater gender equality than much of the rest of India. Without resorting to a coercive approach such as a "one-child policy," Kerala has achieved a rate of population growth lower than China's and also lower than that in some developed countries, including Sweden and Canada.[34] When aid is a means of increasing literacy and gender equality, then it can help achieve a sustainable population.

Still, in poor countries with high fertility rates, more direct measures of slowing fertility may be needed if population is to stabilize at a sustainable level that provides a minimally decent standard of living. But that doesn't reduce the importance of aid, either. Providing basic health care remains central to these efforts, because it is a way of reaching women and talking to them about contraception. If you think that stopping population growth is an overriding priority, you should donate to organizations like Population Services International, or the International Planned Parenthood Federation, asking that your gift be earmarked for family-planning projects.[35]

. . .

When you're a philosopher, and people casually ask you what you do, the next question is likely to be "So what's your philosophy?" My colleague Kwame Anthony Appiah has a good reply: "My philosophy," he says, "is that everything is more complicated than you thought."[36] I don't always agree with Appiah, but working out the likely real-world consequences of aid is often more complicated than we thought, and that is true of any large-scale human activity. Whether the complications involve Dutch disease, bad institutions, or population growth, they introduce an element of uncertainty into our efforts to provide assistance. Nevertheless, some degree of uncertainty about the impact of aid does not eliminate our obligation to give. If an aid project has a good chance of bringing great benefits to the poor, and the cost to us of making that aid project possible is comparatively minor, then we should still give the money.

What we have still not resolved, however, is how much we ought to be giving, especially when we have obligations to our families, and when we are living among people who, in general, give little or nothing. So now, with a firm grounding in human psychology and in the facts about aid, it is time to return to the ethical questions with which we began.

A NEW STANDARD
FOR GIVING

8. Your Child and the Children of Others

Charlotte Perkins Gilman's short story "The Unnatural Mother," first published in 1895, involves a woman faced with a terrible decision. Walking to meet her husband, Esther Greenwood notices that a dam holding back an artificial lake is giving way. She immediately runs to warn those living in the village in the valley below her home, where her baby is sleeping. Rescuing her child will prevent her from getting word to the villagers in time, so she does not stop. She saves the villagers and then returns for her child, but drowns in the attempt, although her child fortunately survives. Old Mrs. Briggs, who has had thirteen children and represents the conventional morality of the day, takes a dim view of Esther's decision. Because she did not put her own child's life ahead of the lives of others, she is an "unnatural mother." Mrs. Briggs's daughter Mary Amelia, through whom Gilman puts forth her own progressive view, points out that Esther saved fifteen hundred lives and was, no doubt, thinking of all the other children at risk. Mrs. Briggs replies that she is ashamed of Mary Amelia for expressing such an opinion: "A mother's duty is to her own child!"

This story raises uncomfortable questions: What is a parent's duty in extreme circumstances? Are there times when our obligation to others is equal to or greater than that to our family? You should love your own children—that goes without saying, and not to do so would be both wrong and unnatural. You must also provide for their needs—feeding, housing, clothing, and educating them. But should you put your own child's life at risk in order to save hundreds of others? Fortunately, few of us will ever be faced with that question. The real dilemma, for most of us, is whether it is wrong and unnatural to reject our children's pleas for the latest expensive computer games, to spurn designer-label kids' clothing, and to send them to the local (entirely adequate but not outstanding) public school rather than the admittedly superior but much more expensive private one. The savings you gain by taking the less-expensive option in each case will allow you to donate substantial sums toward saving the lives of strangers. But do your obligations to your own children override your obligations to strangers, no matter how great their need or suffering?

Zell Kravinsky has been tormented by this very dilemma. Kravinsky has had a busy life: He has taught socially disturbed children in a Philadelphia public school, written two Ph.D. theses, and taught classes on Milton at the University of Pennsylvania. Along the way, he found the time to do enough real estate investing to accumulate, by his mid-forties, a portfolio of shopping malls and other assets worth about $45 million. Conscious of the need to provide for his family, Kravinsky put some money into trust funds for his wife and children, as well as for his sister's children. He then proceeded to give almost all the rest away, retaining only his modest family house in Jenkintown, near Philadelphia, and about $80,000 in stocks and cash. He spends very little on himself; at one point he owned a single suit, bought at a thrift store for $20. As he put it when he visited my class: "It seems to me crystal clear that I should be giving all my money away and donating all my time and energy." In fact giving money, time, and energy wasn't enough for Kravinsky. Learning that thousands of people with failing kidneys die each year while waiting for a transplant, he contacted an inner-city Philadelphia hospital that serves mostly low-income African Americans, and donated one of his kidneys to a stranger.[1]

Kravinsky acknowledged that his wife, Emily, objected to his giving away a kidney on the grounds that one of their children may one day need it. "No matter how infinitesimal the risk to your family," she tells him, "we're your family, and the recipient doesn't count." And this seems like a perfectly reasonable reaction. Most of us put our obligations to our family, especially our children, above everything else. Putting the family first feels natural, and in most cases, it seems right. Kravinsky, however, sees it differently. In his view, "the sacrosanct commitment to the family is the rationalization for all manner of greed and selfishness. Nobody says, 'I'm working for the tobacco company because I like the money.' They say, 'Well, you know, I hate to do it, but I'm saving up for the kids.' Everything is excused that way."

My students are unsettled by Kravinsky's selflessness, particularly when it comes to donating the kidney. He tells them that the chances of dying as a result of doing so are about one in four thousand, and that to withhold a kidney from someone who would otherwise die means that you value your own life four thousand times more highly than that of a stranger, a ratio that he describes as "obscene."

After listening to Kravinsky, a few students are typically led to think seriously about how they might change their own lives, and even entertain the idea of donating a kidney, although to the best of my knowledge none of them has done so. Some respond more defensively, questioning Kravinsky's facts and suggesting that the chances of something going wrong donation or subsequently are higher than one in four (Although Kravinsky's figure accurately states the very ⌐f dying as a result of donating a kidney, some studies have found a much higher risk of nonfatal complications in kidney donors. Nor can success be guaranteed for the recipient, as 5 percent of those who receive a kidney from a living donor die within a year of the operation. That also makes a difference, though only a minor one, to the one-to-four-thousand risk-to-benefit ratio.[2]) Other students, however, begin to question themselves: "Perhaps," they say, "in some sense I do value my own life at more than four thousand times that of a stranger."

Paul Farmer, cofounder of Partners in Health, the organization highly recommended by GiveWell for improving the health care of the rural poor, also feels the conflict between his love for his family and his concern for strangers. Farmer spent a year in Haiti after graduating from college, partly because he knew his money would go a long way there. While working as a volunteer at a Haitian hospital, he became friendly with a young American doctor who had worked in Haiti for a year, but was about to return to the United States. Farmer asked him if it was going to be hard to leave. The doctor replied: "Are you kidding? I can't wait. There's no electricity here. It's just brutal here." Farmer asked: "But aren't you worried about not being able to forget all this? There's so much disease here." The doctor replied that he was an American and he was going home. Farmer says he thought about that response for the rest of the day: "What does that mean, 'I'm an American'?" He wondered why being an American meant that you could forget about the people dying for lack of medical care in Haiti. He knew then that he would become a doctor himself.[3]

Farmer commenced studying for his medical degree at Harvard in 1984, but went back to Haiti on a regular basis, doing research on public health problems in Cange, a town in the central plateau that was poor even by Haitian standards. During this period he met Tom White, the Boston developer who is now a member of the 50% League. Farmer brought White to Haiti to see conditions for himself, and White soon helped him start Partners in Health and became, for its formative years, its principal financial backer. In 1993 the MacArthur Foundation awarded Farmer one of its "genius grants"—$220,000, essentially his to do with as he wished. He donated it all to Partners in Health. After he completed his medical training, he had appointments at Harvard (in medical anthropology) and at the Brigham and Women's Hospital in Boston (in infectious diseases), donating his salary and any royalties or lecture fees to Partners in Health, which paid his bills and added the rest to its funds. As long as he was single, while in Boston he slept in the basement of the Partners in Health headquarters; his house in Cange was so simple it lacked hot water.

Sometimes in Haiti, Farmer will hike for hours to see patients living far from any roads. He insists on doing this because to say that it takes too much time and effort to visit these patients is, in his view, to say that their lives matter less than the lives of others. Flying from the peasant huts and their malnourished babies in Haiti to Miami, just 700 miles away, with its well-dressed people talking about their efforts to lose weight, Farmer gets angry over the contrast between developing countries and the developed world. What troubles him most is the same thing that troubled him all those years ago about the American doctor who was about to leave Haiti: "How people can not care, erase, not remember."

Farmer married Didi Bertrand, the daughter of the schoolmaster in Cange, and when he was thirty-eight, they had a daughter, Catherine. At one point, after failing to save the child of a woman in his clinic who had complications while giving birth, Farmer began to weep. He had to excuse himself and go outside. When he asked himself what was going on, he realized he was crying because he imagined Catherine in the place of the dead baby. "So you love your child more than these kids?" he asked himself. That disturbed him, because he had thought he had complete empathy with the children he was treating, and he saw his inability to love other children as he loved his own as "a failure of empathy." Tracy Kidder, Farmer's biographer, challenged that idea, asking him how he would respond to people who would say: "Where do you get off thinking you're different from everyone and can love the children of others as much as your own?" "Look," Farmer replied, "all the great religious traditions of the world say, 'Love thy neighbor as thyself.' My answer is, I'm sorry, I can't, but I'm gonna keep on trying." As part of that effort, Farmer, who travels a lot and is often away from his family, carries with him a picture of Catherine, and a picture of one of his patients, a Haitian child of about the same age, suffering from malnutrition.

Kidder was with Farmer on one occasion when he visited his wife and child, who were then living in Paris; Didi was studying, in the archives of the French slaveowners, the ordeals of her ancestors. He recounts a poignant moment, shortly after Farmer had arrived, when Farmer was playing with Catherine. Didi, who knew he was traveling on to Moscow, where Partners in Health was involved in an antituberculosis program, asked him when he was leaving. "Tomorrow morning," he replied. In response, Didi, clearly upset, made a deep-throated exclamation—and Farmer covered his mouth with both hands. Kidder writes: "It was the first time I'd seen him at a loss for words or action." If Farmer doesn't spend as much time as he would like with his family, it is because he is driven by the thought: "If I don't work this hard, someone will die who doesn't have to." He just cannot accept the fact that people are dying of diseases for which treatments exist. To him, that's a sin. "One can never work overtime for the poor," he has said. "We're only scrambling to make up for our deficiencies."

Like Farmer, Kravinsky insists that he loves his children as much as any parent, and I am convinced that he does. He protected them from his own commitment to others by setting up a trust fund for them. But his fatherly love does not, in his view, justify his placing a value on their lives thousands of times greater than the value he places on the lives of the children of strangers. Pressed by Ian Parker, who was writing about him for *The New Yorker,* to calculate a ratio between his love for his children and his love for unknown children, Kravinsky replied: "I don't know where I'd set it, but I would not let many children die so my kids could live," and then added: "I don't think that two kids should die so that one of my kids has comfort, and I don't know that two children should die so that one of my kids lives."[4]

Parker could not ask the fictional Mrs. Briggs for her opinion of Kravinsky's attitude, but he seems to have found the next best thing in MIT philosopher Judith Jarvis Thomson, who commented: "A father who says, 'I'm no more concerned about my children's lives than about anybody else's life,' is just flatly a defective parent; he's deficient in views that parents ought to have, whether it maximizes utility or not." Kravinsky didn't, in fact, say that he is no more concerned about his children's lives than anybody else's life, though he came closer to that than most people would. Does that make him a defective parent? Children do need loving parents. They need to feel that their parents will protect them and stick by them. Children might well be disturbed to discover that their father would allow them to die so that the children of strangers can be saved. Yet literature is full of situations in which parents must choose between their child and some broader moral imperative, and in considering these situations we don't always assume that parents ought to put their children first. If we did, it is hard to see how Abraham could be honored, as he is in the Jewish, Christian, and Islamic religions, for his readiness to obey God's command that he sacrifice Isaac, his only son.[5] The ancient Greeks, too, considered that a father might have to sacrifice a child for a greater good. In Euripides' play *Iphigeneia at Aulis,* the Greek fleet is ready to sail for Troy, but the goddess Artemis will not provide a favorable wind unless Agamemnon, the Greek leader, sacrifices his daughter Iphigeneia. Agamemnon vows that he loves his children: "Only the mad do not." Yet he tells his daughter: "It is Greece that compels me to sacrifice you, whatever I wish." If we are less sympathetic to Agamemnon than to Abraham, perhaps that is because today Jews, Christians, and Muslims still worship the god of Abraham, but who believes in the gods of the ancient Greeks?

The limits to what a mother may do to save the life of her child are probed in a more recent setting in Joseph Kanon's novel *The Good German.* In the aftermath of World War II, Renate Naumann, a German Jewish woman, is on trial for collaborating with the Nazis in the despicable role of a *greifer,* someone who identifies Jews living as non-Jews. We learn that if she had refused, or failed to meet her quota, Naumann's own life, and that of her elderly mother, would have been at risk, but we do not think that that excuses her. Then there is a surprise twist. We discover that Naumann has a son, hidden away from the Nazis, who could not have survived without her. Does that make her collaboration acceptable? Would she have been a defective parent if she had *not* put her son's life ahead of the lives of strangers?

We tend to think that people are more to blame for their acts than for their omissions. That may be why we are much more ready to condemn Naumann for saving her child than we would be to denounce a woman who, in Esther Greenwood's situation, chose to save her own child at the cost of omitting to warn hundreds of others. Still, if we do condemn Renate Naumann, we are putting limits on what you may do to save your own child. We then have to ask whether these limits are not also breached by choosing the act that saves your own child but allows other people's children to die.

As I see them, neither Esther Greenwood nor Zell Kravin-sky nor Paul Farmer is a defective parent. They love their chil-dren and want to protect them. Their problem is that they are also pulled by the needs of others in a way that most people are not. Like Abraham and Agamemnon, they are anguished over a choice that others make on the basis of their feelings alone, neither empathizing with others' needs nor trying to take a less partial perspective. Recently, in response to his wife's concerns and because he did not want to be estranged from his children, Kravinsky went back into real estate, made more money, and bought his family a larger home. When it came to the crunch, he was, after all, a "natural father" who chose to keep the fam-ily together. We might say that even he could not resist the power of the norm of self-interest, although it was the power the norm had over his family, combined with the special love he has for them, that forced his retreat from putting an equal value on all lives.

Although Farmer holds himself to an extremely demanding moral standard, he is realistic about what he expects from oth-ers. I've heard him speak to students, attracting a capacity crowd, many of them fervent admirers—hero-worshippers, almost—but he does not challenge them to do as he does. He doesn't take vacations, but he encourages others working for Partners in Health to take them. He won't spend money on luxuries, but he doesn't express disapproval of others who do, as long as they also give something to the poor. Perhaps that is because he realizes that it's important to, as Partners in Health cofounder Jim Kim told Tracy Kidder, "make sure people are inspired by him. But we can't say anybody should or could be just like him. Because if the poor have to wait for a lot of peo-ple like Paul to come along before they get good health care, they are totally fucked." What this suggests is that we may need to set our standards lower in order to draw more people to meet them.

Chuck Collins, cofounder of Responsible Wealth, member

of the 50% League, and grandson of Oscar Mayer, has felt the pressure of family obligations push against his desire to do the most good he can with his wealth, even though he gave away most of his money before he even had children. "People would say, 'That's fine, you can be reckless in your own life, but you shouldn't do that to your children.' " Collins's answer was that parents make decisions for their children all the time, and that deciding that they will not inherit wealth is one of those decisions. He firmly believes that inherited wealth is not good for children—that's one of the arguments Responsible Wealth uses for retaining the estate tax. But Collins doesn't go to extremes: "Of course, we have to respond to our immediate family, but, once they're okay, we need to expand the circle. A larger sense of family is a radical idea, but we get into trouble as a society when we don't see that we're in the same boat."[6]

That seems a reasonable stance, and one not too violently at odds with human nature, but of course "okay" is a very vague notion. My students often ask me if I think their parents did wrong to pay the $44,000 per year that it costs to send them to Princeton. I respond that paying that much for a place at an elite university is not justified unless it is seen as an investment in the future that will benefit not only one's child, but others as well. An outstanding education provides students with the skills, qualifications, and understanding to do more for the world than would otherwise be the case. It is good for the world as a whole if there are more people with these qualities. Even if going to Princeton does no more than open doors to jobs with higher salaries, that, too, is a benefit that can be spread to others, as long as after graduating you remain firm in the resolve to contribute a percentage of that salary to organizations working for the poor, and spread this idea among your highly paid colleagues. The danger, of course, is that your colleagues will instead persuade you that you can't possibly drive anything less expensive than a BMW and that you absolutely must live in an impressively large apartment in one of the most expensive parts of town.

When discussing with Kidder his inability to love other children as much as he loves his own daughter, Farmer comments: "The thing is, everybody understands that, encourages that, praises you for it. But the hard thing is the other." He's right, of course. It is much harder to love the children of strangers than to love your own children. Yet as a society, we encourage parents to love and care for their children because that is the way to bring up happy, psychologically healthy children. There is no better way of doing it. Some utopian communities have attempted to replace the family tie with an ethic of commitment to the whole community, but even the most enlightened of these efforts, like the Israeli kibbutzim, found that the bond between parents and children was too strong to suppress. Parents would sneak into the children's house to cuddle their children, and some studies suggested that children brought up communally found it difficult to make deep emotional attachments.[7] Gradually, the kibbutzim brought back the nuclear family, acknowledging that the attempt to separate children from their parents and bring them up collectively was a failure. For that reason the conflict that Farmer and Kravinsky feel so acutely, between being an ideal parent and acting on the idea that all human life is of equal value, is real and irresolvable. The two will always be in tension. No principle of obligation is going to be widely accepted unless it recognizes that parents will and should love their own children more than the children of strangers, and, for that reason, will meet the basic needs of their children before they meet the needs of strangers. But this doesn't mean that parents are justified in providing luxuries for their children ahead of the basic needs of others.

9. Asking Too Much?

In the first part of this book I argued that in order to be good people, we must give until if we gave more, we would be sacrificing something nearly as important as the bad things our donation can prevent. Now that we have a better idea of what our donation can prevent, it's time to return and probe more deeply the sense that there *must* be something amiss with this moral argument because its implications go too far. Almost all of us spend money on things we don't need; to be ethical, do we really have to give them up? Exploring different views of our ethical obligations that stop short of such demanding conclusions will help us decide.

A Fair Share

We saw earlier that our sense of fairness provides us with a powerful motivation against doing more than our fair share. But does the fact that giving as much as the earlier argument suggests would involve us in doing more than our fair share also provide us with a moral justification for not overstepping the limits of what our fair share might be? Philosophers Liam Murphy and Kwame Anthony Appiah both answer this question affirmatively.[1] They agree that the world's affluent people are obliged to provide enough aid to eliminate large-scale extreme poverty. But this is, in their view, an obligation that we have as a group. Each member of the group is responsible for his or her fair share, and no more. As Appiah puts it in his *Cosmopolitanism,* "If so many people in the world are not doing their share—and they clearly are not—it seems to me I cannot be required to derail my life to take up the slack."[2]

Just to see what this view would imply, let us assume, for the moment, that Murphy and Appiah are right. What would your fair share be? If we knew the amount of aid needed to ensure that the world's poorest people have a chance at a decent life, and divided that figure by the number of affluent people in a position to contribute something, this would tell you how much you need to donate to do your fair share of meeting our obligation to the poor.

One very crude way of calculating this figure is to estimate by how much the income of the world's poor falls below the poverty line, and then calculate how much money it would take to move all the poor above this line, to the level at which they have enough income to meet their basic needs. Jeffrey Sachs did this and concluded that in 2001 it would have taken $124 billion a year to raise everyone above the poverty line. The combined gross annual income of the twenty-two rich OECD nations in that year was $20 trillion. Therefore the contribution needed to make up the shortfall is 0.62 percent of income, or 62 cents of every $100 earned. A person making $50,000 per year would owe just over $300. This is hardly a crippling sum. By comparison, in 1999 Americans spent $116 billion on alcohol.[3] Giving just half of this to the poor would cover all Americans' share of what needs to be done, and still allow those who enjoy a drink to have one or two.[4]

The calculation, however, is too crude: Neither Sachs nor anyone else is seriously proposing that we solve world poverty by handing poor people enough money to meet their basic needs. That would not be likely to produce a lasting solution to the many problems that the poor face.

To get an idea of the kind of sum needed for reducing poverty in a more sustainable manner, we can take as our target, at least until 2015, the Millennium Development Goals agreed to by leaders of all the world's nations at the UN Millennium Development Summit held in New York in 2000. These goals, chosen because they were challenging but feasible targets to be reached by 2015, include:

- Reducing by half the proportion of the world's people in extreme poverty

- Reducing by half the proportion of people who suffer from hunger

- Ensuring that children everywhere are able to take a full course of primary schooling

- Ending sex disparity in education

- Reducing by two-thirds the mortality rate among children under five

- Reducing by three quarters the rate of maternal mortality

- Halting and beginning to reverse the spread of HIV/AIDS and halting and beginning to reduce the incidence of malaria and other major diseases

- Reducing by half the proportion of people without sustainable access to safe drinking water

A United Nations task force, again headed by Sachs, estimated how much it would cost to meet these goals. The task force drew on preliminary assessments in Bangladesh, Cambodia, Ghana, Tanzania, and Uganda that suggested that the development goals could be achieved for a per capita annual cost of $70 to $80 in 2006, increasing, as projects are gradually scaled up, to $120 to $160 in 2015. On that basis, the task force reached a global estimate—which the task force warns is provisional, but believes is of "the right order of magnitude"— of $121 billion in 2006, rising to $189 billion by 2015.[5] When we take account of existing official development aid promises, the additional amount needed each year to meet the goals is only $48 billion for 2006 and $74 billion for 2015.

Now we can calculate how much each affluent person would have to contribute for the combined sum to meet these totals and achieve these results. According to Branko Milanovic of the World Bank, if we define the "rich" as those who have an income above the average income of Portugal (the lowest-income nation in the "rich club" of western Europe, North America, Japan, Australia, and New Zealand) then there are 855 million rich people in the world.[6] If each of us gave $200 per year, that would total $171 billion, or roughly the amount Sachs's United Nations task force believes is needed each year to meet the Millennium Development Goals. These goals, as we have just seen, seek merely to halve global poverty, not to eliminate it. But let us put that aside for the moment; to achieve the goals by 2015 would be a good start on the way to eliminating widespread global poverty.

Among those 855 million rich people, some are barely above the average income of Portugal, and others are billionaires. It doesn't seem fair that they should all have to give the same amount; it would be better to use a sliding scale, like a tax scale, with the truly rich giving not only a larger sum, but also a greater percentage of their income than those who are no more than average wage earners in an affluent country. In the final chapter, I suggest a sliding scale reflecting this version of fairness. For the moment, however we can ignore the details, and focus instead on the fact that if everyone were doing their fair share, the total amount each of us would need to give in order to wipe out, or at least drastically reduce, large-scale extreme poverty would be in the hundreds, rather than thousands, of dollars per year.

Just a reminder of what this would do. The task force described the benefits that will result from meeting the Millennium Development Goals. As compared with a "business as usual" scenario, meeting the goals will mean that 500 million fewer people are living in extreme poverty and 300 million people will no longer suffer from hunger. There will be 350 million fewer without safe drinking water, and 650 million people will gain basic sanitation. Over the coming decade, the lives of 30 million children will be saved, and 2 million fewer women will die as a result of pregnancy and childbirth. In addition, millions of children will have increased opportunities because they have been able to attend school, and environmental degradation will be slowed or reversed.

But most people are not doing their fair share, so we still need to ask: Is our fair share really all that each of us is obliged to do. Here's yet another version of the pond story to help us think about this question. You are walking past the shallow pond when you see that ten children have fallen in and need to be rescued. Glancing around, you see no parents or caregivers, but you do notice that, as well as yourself, there are nine adults who have just arrived at the pond, have also seen the drowning children, and are in as good a position as you to rescue a child. So you rush into the water, grab a child, and place him safely away from the water. You look up, expecting that every other adult will have done the same, and all the children will therefore be safe, but to your dismay you see that while four other adults have each rescued a child, the other five just strolled on. In the pond there are still five children, apparently about to drown. The "fair-share" theorists would say that you have now done your fair share of the rescuing. If everyone had done what you did, all of the children would have been saved. Since no one is in a better position to rescue a child than anyone else, your fair share of the task is simply to rescue one child, and you are under no obligation to do more than that. But is it acceptable for you and the other four adults to stop after you have rescued just one child each, knowing that this means that five children will drown?

This question really amounts to asking: Is the fact that other people are not doing their fair share a sufficient reason for allowing a child to die when you could easily rescue that child? I think the answer is clear: No. The others have, by refusing to help with the rescue, made themselves irrelevant. They might as well be so many rocks. According to the fair-share view, in fact, it would be better for the children if they *were* rocks, because then you would be obliged to wade back into the pond to save another child. It is not the fault of the children whose lives are at risk that there are other people who could help rescue them but are refusing to do their fair share. The action or inaction of these people cannot make it right for us to let children drown when we could easily save them.[7]

Liam Murphy thinks that if you do save one child in this situation, and then refuse to save a second one, you have done nothing wrong. He seeks to explain away the apparent implausibility of this view by saying that your refusal to save the second child when you could have easily rescued him shows that you have an "appalling character," but not that you have done anything wrong. We might, he says, shun a person who can show such emotional indifference to the pressing needs of a specific person in danger of drowning.[8] But it isn't just the person's character that is a problem, it is that he has allowed a child to die when he could have easily rescued that child. What he has done is appalling. He's like a child who stamps his foot and says "It's *not fair!*" A sense of fairness is, as we've seen, advantageous for individuals and for the society in which they live, and is probably innate, but when we grow up, we learn that sometimes we have to accept unfairness. We don't have to like it, and we can certainly rail against the person not doing his share; but in most circumstances, we'll do what has to be done if the costs of not doing so are high enough. Those who refuse as a matter of principle to do more than their fair share make a fetish of fairness. It's like having an absolute stance on lying, even in a case where telling a lie would save an innocent person from being murdered. While in both cases—fairness and lying—it's almost always important to maintain the principle, there are times when doing so is simply wrong.

This doesn't prove that fairness makes no difference. The example of saving more drowning children than your fair share would require is not one in which, to use Appiah's phrase, I must "derail my life" in order to make up for what others leave undone. Perhaps in saving lives when others are not doing their share, I am obliged to go beyond what strict fairness requires, but I can justifiably stop before I reach the point at which I am sacrificing something nearly as important as the life I am saving. It's difficult to say just what weight, if any, we should give to fairness in such a situation. But even if we grant Appiah's claim that we are not required to derail our lives to make up for the deficiencies of others, his position may still require us to do a lot more than most of us do now.

A Moderately Demanding View

If we can dismiss the argument that limits our obligations to our fair share, the next challenge is to examine a number of more-demanding standards that have arisen in recent philosophical debates. According to Richard Miller, a philosopher who has written widely about global justice, we ought to give to the point at which, if we were to give more, we would run a "significant" risk of worsening our lives—but we do not need to go beyond this point. Miller's idea is that morality allows us to pursue "the underlying goals to which we are securely attached" but that, when others are in need, it does not allow us to spend more than we need to achieve those goals.[9] Garrett Cullity, author of *The Moral Demands of Affluence,* believes that we should give to the point at which further contributions would undermine our pursuit of "intrinsically life-enhancing goods" such as friendship, developing one's musical talents, and being involved in the life of one's community.[10] In his book *Ideal Code, Real World,* Brad Hooker argues that we should try to live according to the code that, if widely accepted, would lead to the best outcome. Hooker asserts that we are morally required to help those in greater need "even if the personal sacrifices involved in helping them add up to a significant cost," but that we are not required to go beyond this threshold.[11]

Miller's standard is the least demanding. If it is important to you to express your sense of who you are by occasionally buying clothes or accessories that are stylish or fun, rather than something more basic, you are permitted to buy those items. The same is true of eating: If we never ate in good restaurants we could not pursue our "worthwhile" goal of eating "in a way that explores a variety of interesting aesthetic and cultural possibilities." Similarly, enjoying "the capacity of great composers and performers to exploit nuances of timbre and texture to powerful aesthetic effect" is a worthwhile goal, and one that justifies buying "more than minimal" stereo equipment.

Cullity's standard is more demanding. His "intrinsically life-enhancing goods" don't appear to include things like stylish clothes, though they do include whatever is necessary to enjoy music, since he regards that as an intrinsically life-enhancing good. But for most goods, if there is a cheaper alternative I can pursue that is not substantially worse for me, that is what I should go for. Only goods like friendship and integrity, which involve our deepest commitments, should not be judged on the basis of how much they cost.

Hooker acknowledges that his criterion is vague, but says it would be met by a person who regularly gives a little money or time to charities. He stresses that the test is whether all of the time or money given adds up to a significant cost, not whether the sacrifice involved on any particular occasion of helping someone in greater need is significant. Hence giving to this level would not require forgoing, Hooker says, one's personal projects.

So our obligations to the poor do not, in Miller, Cullity, and Hooker's views, go as far as to say that you must give to the point where if you give any more, you will be sacrificing something nearly as important as a child's life. However, it's important not to lose sight of the fact that these three philosophers agree that if you fail to give anything, or give only trivial sums to aid the world's poorest people, you are acting wrongly. Depending on the facts about how much it would take to overcome widespread extreme poverty, the obligations Miller, Cullity, and Hooker posit may be considerably more demanding than the fair-share view. Miller, for example, would allow us to purchase a luxury item of attire "only occasionally." The stereo that the music lover may buy can be "more than minimal," but that implies that we are not justified in buying at the top of the line, even if we can afford it. Cullity allows us to spend money on significant activities that will enhance our lives, but spending on trivial items should, in his view, be redirected to helping combat poverty. Hooker says you are required to give to those in greater need to the point at which the total of the money or time you have given involves a significant personal cost. Against the background of a world in which most affluent people give only a trivial proportion of their income, or none at all, to help the poor, the agreement among the four of us that we all have, at a minimum, moderately demanding obligations to help the poor is more important than the differences between us.

Many people get great pleasure from dressing stylishly, eating well, and listening to music on a good stereo system. I'm all for pleasure—the more the better, other things being equal. There's no denying that there is value in the things that Miller, Cullity, and Hooker think we are entitled to spend our money on. But my argument does imply that it is wrong to spend money on those things when we could instead be using the money to save people's lives and prevent great suffering. The problem is that we are living in the midst of an emergency in which 27,000 children die from avoidable causes every day. That's more than one thousand every hour. And millions of women are living with repairable fistulas, and millions of people are blind who could see again. We can do something about these things. That crucial fact ought to affect the choices we make. To buy good stereo equipment in order to further my worthwhile goal, or life-enhancing experience, of listening to music is to place more value on these enhancements to my life than on whether others live or die. Can it be ethical to live that way? Doesn't it make a mockery of any claim to believe in the equal value of human life?

For the same reason, philanthropy for the arts or for cultural activities is, in a world like this one, morally dubious. In 2004, New York's Metropolitan Museum of Art paid a sum said to be in excess of $45 million for a small Madonna and Child painted by the medieval Italian master Duccio. In buying this painting, the museum has added to the abundance of masterpieces that those fortunate enough to be able to visit it can see. But if it only costs $50 to perform a cataract operation in a developing country, that means there are 900,000 people who can't see anything at all, let alone a painting, whose sight could have been restored by the amount of money that painting cost. At $450 to repair a fistula, $45 million could have given 100,000 women another chance at a decent life. At $1,000 a life, it could have saved 45,000 lives—a football stadium full of people. How can a painting, no matter how beautiful and historically significant, compare with that? If the museum were on fire, would anyone think it right to save the Duccio from the flames, rather than a child? And that's just one child. In a world in which more-pressing needs had already been met, philanthropy for the arts would be a noble act. Sadly, we don't live in such a world.

So neither the "fair-share" view, nor any of these more moderate views, gives us a tenable answer to the question "What ought I to do to help those in great need?" Nevertheless, I think that these views do have a place in answering a different practical question, to which I now turn.

10. A Realistic Approach

Faced with an ethical argument that requires us to give away much of our income, we might ask whether there is any point to a standard that cuts so strongly against the grain of human nature that virtually no one follows it. Over many years of talking and writing about this subject, I have found that for some people, striving for a high moral standard pushes them in the right direction, even if they—and here I include myself—do not go as far as the standard implies they should. The research by Shang and Croson referred to in chapter 5, on how the amount donated by callers to American public radio stations can be increased by telling them about large amounts given by others, suggests the same conclusion. But Shang and Croson found that the method worked only within limits. Asking people to give more than almost anyone else gives risks turning them off, and at some level might cause them to question the point of striving to live an ethical life at all. Daunted by what it takes to do the right thing, they may ask themselves why they are bothering to try. To avoid that danger, we should advocate a level of giving that will lead to a positive response. Because I want to see those in poverty receive as much as possible of the aid they need, I think we should advocate the level of giving that will raise the largest possible total, and so have the best consequences.

In this chapter, I propose a much easier target: roughly 5 percent of annual income for those who are financially comfortable, and rather more for the very rich. My hope is that people will be convinced that they can and should give at this level. I believe that doing so would be a first step toward restoring the ethical importance of giving as an essential component of a well-lived life. And if it is widely adopted, we'll have more than enough money to end extreme poverty.

I concede that this standard falls far short of the moral argument I put forward earlier, for it remains true, of course, that most people could, after giving 5 percent of their income to reduce global poverty, give more without sacrificing anything nearly as important as the lives they would be saving. So how can I now say that people who give 5 percent are fulfilling their obligations when they are still far from doing what my argument concludes they ought to be doing? The reason lies in the difference between what I ought to do, as an individual, and what set of principles, or moral code, I should advocate and seek to have acted upon by most people in our society.

Take the basic argument that torture is always wrong. Given the well-documented tendency of police and guards to abuse prisoners, and the low probability that torture will yield useful information, that rule seems likely to have the best consequences. Yet, I would argue, if I find myself in the highly improbable scenario where only torturing a terrorist will enable me to stop a nuclear bomb from going off in the middle of New York City, I ought to torture the terrorist. What the individual ought to do, and what the best moral rule directs one to do, are not necessarily identical.

Some philosophers deny that there can be a gap between what we believe we ought to do and the general moral rules we ought to advocate; in their view, it is always wrong to do what you cannot publicly advocate as a rule for everyone to follow. They want everything up front and transparent. Kant famously wrote that the test of whether an action is right is whether you can prescribe that the principle on which it is based should be a universal law.[1] John Rawls drew on this idea when he made "the publicity condition" a key element of his theory of justice.[2] That sounds like a fine idea, but it overlooks the fact that to be widely accepted and acted upon, as we wish them to be, moral rules have to be attuned to our evolved human nature, with all its quirky relics of our tribal past. If we fail to take into account the biases that, as we saw in chapter 4, make it difficult to persuade us to give anything like the same weight to the interests of distant people we cannot identify as we give to the interests of people we can see or name, then the moral rules we advocate will do little good, because few people will follow them. I am in a different situation, however, when I am making my own decision about how much to give. I can't then appeal to my own human nature as a reason for not doing what I would otherwise judge that I ought to do. As the French existentialist philosopher Jean-Paul Sartre famously pointed out, when I ask myself what I *ought* to do, I am free. It would simply not be true for me to say: "I can't give a thousand dollars to help strangers in Africa, because I'm human and humans are less concerned about distant anonymous strangers than they are about people nearby whom they know." How does that stop me from going to Oxfam's website, filling in my credit card details, and donating $1,000? How does it even provide a reason against it? I would, to use one of the existentialists' favorite terms of condemnation, be "lacking in authenticity" if I were to appeal to human nature as a reason for not doing what I see to be right, and what nothing is preventing me from doing, except that I do not choose to do it.

If this still sounds puzzling, it is in part because we are used to thinking of morality in simple black-and-white terms. You either do what is right, and deserve to be praised, or you do what is wrong, and should be blamed. But moral life is more nuanced than that suggests. We use praise and blame to influence behavior, and the appropriate standard must be relative to what we can reasonably expect most people to do. Hence praise and blame, at least when they are given publicly, should follow the standard that we publicly advocate, not the higher standard that we might apply to our own conduct. We should praise people for doing significantly better than most people in their circumstances would do, and blame them for doing significantly worse. If you have done more than your fair share, that must at least lessen the blame. If you have complied with the public moral code, we should praise you for doing that, rather than blame you for not doing more.[3]

Judging the Rich and Famous

This brings us back to the world's wealthiest people, many of whom give away tremendous amounts of money to charity. How should we think about Bill Gates, who gave $29 billion to fighting poverty, but remains one of the world's richest people?

Gates knows what the ultimate standard is. It's prominent on the Bill and Melinda Gates Foundation website: "All lives—no matter where they are being led—have equal value." Gates says that he got started in philanthropy when he read that half a million children die every year from rotavirus. He had never heard of rotavirus. (It is the most common cause of severe diarrhea in children.) He asked himself: "How could I never have heard of something that kills half a million children every year?" He then learned that in developing countries, millions of children die from diseases that have been eliminated, or virtually eliminated, in the United States. That shocked him, because he had assumed that if there are vaccines and treatments that could save lives, governments would be doing everything possible to get them to the people who need them. As Gates tells the story, he and his wife, Melinda, "couldn't escape the brutal conclusion that—in our world today—some lives are seen as worth saving and others are not." They said to themselves, "This can't be true." But they knew it was.[4] This led Gates to set up the foundation, to endow it with an initial gift of $28.8 billion, and, since 2008, to devote himself full-time to making it as effective as possible.

Gates's gift was, at the time, the largest philanthropic donation ever made, dwarfing the lifetime contributions of Carnegie or Rockefeller, even when adjusted for inflation. (Warren Buffett has since pledged to give a billion or two more than Gates has given so far, but Gates is continuing to give, and it isn't yet possible to say who will eventually give more.) Gates deserves to be commended for his generosity and for the farsighted way in which he has chosen the goals and methodology of his foundation. Yet for all his generosity, it's obvious that Gates doesn't live by the idea of the equal value of all human life. His 50,000-square-foot high-tech lakeside house near Seattle has been estimated to be worth $135 million. Property taxes amount to nearly $1 million.[5] Among Gates's possessions is the Codex Leicester, the only handwritten book by Leonardo da Vinci still in private hands, for which he paid $30.8 million in 1994. So should we praise him for exceeding, by a long way, what most people, including most of the superrich, give, or should we blame him for living in luxury while others still die from preventable diseases? He could give more, and it's to be hoped that he still will, but I think we should praise him for giving as much as he has.

We should use the same comparative standard to judge celebrities who help the poor. In 2006, when Madonna adopted her son David, then a sickly one-year-old living in an orphanage in Malawi, the media attacked her. The boy's father, they discovered, was alive, so they rushed the television cameras out to him; he gave an interview in which he appeared not to fully understand the legal significance of adoption. But David's father had been unable to care for him after David's mother died, and had placed him in the orphanage. Largely because of Malawi's HIV/AIDS epidemic, the country has a million such orphans. Resources at the orphanages are limited, and many of the children do not live to their fifth birthday. Madonna said that when she met David, he had severe pneumonia and was breathing with difficulty. Malawi is one of the world's poorest countries, with an infant mortality rate of ninety-four per one thousand and a life expectancy at birth of forty-one years. Of the adult population, about one in seven has HIV/AIDS. Had David been left in the orphanage, there is no reason to think that he would have done better than the average Malawian. Most likely, he would have done much worse.

In adopting a child from a poor country, Madonna is following an example set by other celebrities, among them Mia Farrow, Ewan McGregor, and Angelina Jolie. Adoptions have the appeal of an identifiable beneficiary like "Rokia" but they fail to address the causes of poverty. If that were all these celebrities were doing, we might guess that the adoptions are more for their own benefit than for that of the world's poorest children. To her credit, though, Madonna is doing more than adopting David. Raising Malawi, a charity she cofounded, raises money to help orphans in Malawi, to support education for girls, and to gather funds for Jeffrey Sachs's Millennium Villages Project. Angelina Jolie also supports Millennium Villages, while Natalie Imbruglia is a spokesperson for the Campaign to End Fistula. I do not know what percentage of their time or income these stars give to the fight against global poverty and its consequences, but if it is significantly more than most movie or pop stars, we should praise them for what they do rather than focus on how much more they could do.

On the other hand, for those among the superrich who live with particular extravagance and give relatively little, some blame would not be out of order. Consider Paul Allen, sometimes called the "accidental zillionaire." In 1975, Allen got together with a high school friend to start a computer company. Eight years later, he parted from his friend, but held on to about a quarter of the company's stock. The erstwhile friend was Bill Gates, and the company was Microsoft. Now *Forbes* lists Allen's net worth as $16 billion.[6] That's about a quarter of what Gates had when he gave away $28.8 billion. According to Allen's website he has, over his lifetime, given away more than $900 million to philanthropic causes. Very few people will ever be able to give that much, but it's less than one-thirtieth of what Gates has given away, and compares poorly with what most comparably megarich give.[7] Moreover, in contrast to the projects Gates is founding, Allen has focused his limited philanthropy on arts foundations, hospitals, and other community projects in the already-wealthy Pacific Northwest of the United States, where he lives. Nor is Allen living modestly and investing his fortune to give away at some future time, as Buffett did. He owns three professional sports teams, into which he has poured hundreds of millions of dollars. His toys include a large collection of vintage military aircraft and a 413-foot oceangoing yacht called *Octopus* that cost him over $200 million and has a permanent crew of sixty. When launched in 2003, *Octopus* was the world's largest yacht. It has its own music studio and basketball court, two helicopters, seven boats, a submarine, and a remote-controlled vehicle for observing the ocean floor. The submarine can sleep eight for up to two weeks underwater, if that is what you fancy. According to Yachtcrew, a website for those seeking careers on yachts, owners typically must spend a minimum of 10 percent of the vessel's cost every year to keep it in good working condition and cover crew salaries. And Allen owns two other monster yachts, including *Tatoosh,* which in 2003 was the world's third largest.[8]

I don't know Paul Allen, and I hope that what I have written about him will not be seen as a personal attack. His lifestyle is, rather, symptomatic of our culture, and it is that culture that I wish to criticize. After all, Allen isn't alone in enjoying such toys. *Octopus* has now slipped to sixth place in size, behind yachts owned by royalty from Dubai and Saudi Arabia, the Russian billionaire Roman Abramovich, and Larry Ellison, the chief executive officer of the software company Oracle. Ellison is another extravagant billionaire who could be doing a lot more good with his money; he has been quoted as saying "Money is just a method of keeping score." Currently ranking at fourteen on *Forbes's* list of the world's richest, he is estimated to be worth $25 billion. He has a forty-acre Japanese-style estate in Woodside, California, estimated to be worth $200 million, and properties in Malibu worth more than $180 million. He put millions of dollars of his own money into unsuccessful bids to challenge for the 2003 and 2007 America's Cup. He owns many exotic cars and several planes, including fighter jets. His yacht *Rising Sun* cost about $200 million to build— about the same as Allen's *Octopus,* but he complains that it is hard to find berths big enough for it, and so he has now ordered a smaller "leisure yacht" that will be easier to park. According to *Slate,* in 2007 he gave away $39 million. If that sounds generous, think of it this way: If Ellison never earned another dollar, he could give away $39 million every year for the next six hundred years and still have more than $1 billion as a cushion for his old age.[9]

Vitellius, the Roman emperor, dined on the brains of thousands of peacocks and the tongues of thousands of flamingos. Today we regard that as evidence of moral depravity. We could say the same about those who own these megayachts. If that seems a harsh judgment ("No flamingos died in the making of this yacht"), consider first the incredible extravagance involved in buying and maintaining such vessels. Now that you have the figures, do the sums for yourself and calculate how many women's lives could have been restored by surgery to repair their fistulas, how many blind people could have been enabled to see, and how many children could have been saved from dying from malaria for the cost of building *Rising Sun* or *Octopus,* and for the cost of running either each year. But that isn't all; the awkward facts of climate change also condemn those who own large private yachts. Don't be fooled by the name: These vessels aren't wind-powered, they are ships with big engines that churn through incredible quantities of diesel fuel and pump the resulting greenhouse gases into the atmosphere. Ellison's *Rising Sun,* for example, is powered by four engines, each of which, at full power, consumes 548 gallons of fuel per hour, making a total of 2,192 gallons per hour for the ship. In a single hour, *Rising Sun* burns up as much diesel as the average American driver would need to drive a diesel-powered Volkswagen Jetta for seven years.[10] In terms of smog-inducing nitrogen oxide emissions, the yacht engines are even worse: It would take the average American driver twenty years to drive a Jetta far enough to equal the nitrogen oxide emissions that *Rising Sun* emits in an hour. And all that fuel is being burned up not so that people can grow food, or get to work, or visit their loved ones, but so that Larry Ellison can amuse himself and show off how rich he is. It's time we stopped thinking of these ways of spending money as silly but harmless displays of vanity, and started thinking of them as evidence of a grievous lack of concern for others. We need an ethical culture that takes account of the consequences of what each of us does for the world in which we are living, and that judges accordingly.

The Public Standard

This brings us to the important question of what the public standard for giving—as opposed to a higher standard we might privately follow—should be. Some groups have already made an effort to set such a standard, and many people have developed standards of their own.

James Hong became a millionaire at thirty-two after founding Hot or Not?, a phenomenally popular website that allows people to upload their photos and be rated by strangers on a scale of one to ten. Though pleased by his success, Hong didn't want to become part of the Silicon Valley rat race. He told a *New York Times* interviewer: "There is no 'winning' because there will always be someone who has more than you." The way around that, Hong decided, is to give money away instead of accumulating it. But how much to give? He asked other friends among the founders and early employees of successful Internet start-ups around the San Francisco Bay area, where he lives, and received widely varying answers. He settled on a formula: Give 10 percent of everything you earn over $100,000. To encourage others to do the same, he set up a website called 10over100, and on it pledged that he would always give according to the 10over100 rule. The website invites others to make the same pledge. Last time I checked, 3,967 had done so.[11]

Israel Shenker, founder and CEO of the Philadelphia-based real estate firm ISS Development, is happy to tell others about his standard. He matches everything he spends on discretionary items—vacations, a luxury car, a larger house than he needs—with a charitable donation of the same amount.

Fair Share International, an organization based in Adelaide, Australia, is a community of people committed to following a "5.10.5.10" formula. This means:

- Donating 5 percent of your gross annual income to help the disadvantaged

- Reducing your environmentally harmful consumption by 10 percent each year until you can do no more
- Giving 5 percent of your time to helping people in your community
- Taking democratic political action at least 10 times a year, for example, contacting your political representatives

Each of these standards has broader appeal than the much more demanding requirement for membership in the 50% League. If you are not rich, 10over100 will be the easiest to meet, because it demands nothing at all until you earn $100,000 a year, and if you earn, say, $120,000 you will still be giving less than 2 percent of your total income. On the other hand, if you earn a million, you will give 9 percent of your total income, which is a more respectable sum. But many people earning less than $100,000 are able to give and would want to do so, especially if they saw that others are contributing. Shenker's standard is a self-imposed consumption tax—if you spend extravagantly, you will also be giving substantially. But much will depend on how strictly the category of "discretionary item" is interpreted: Remember that bottle of water. On the other hand, a consumption-related standard allows those who are reinvesting their income productively to live modestly and continue to do so. The very rich, though, should go beyond merely matching their philanthropy to their consumption. If you earn $100 million a year, you would need to have lavish tastes to spend more than 10 percent of your earnings, and you could easily give more than that. Fair Share International offers a rule of thumb for how the ethical twenty-first-century citizen should live, covering not only how much we should give but also how much time we should devote to good causes and how sustainable our lifestyle should be. At 5 percent, its suggested level of giving is suitable for those of average means, but again, quite low for anyone who is seriously rich.

The more you earn, the easier it should be to give, not only in terms of dollars, but also as a percentage of your income. If you earn $500,000, giving 5 percent is no hardship at all. It still leaves you with $475,000, which should be enough for anyone. If you earn only $50,000 and are supporting a family, however, finding a spare $2,500 to give away might be tough. So the suggestion that you should give 5 percent of your gross income demands a lot from people on incomes that are, for an affluent nation, relatively low, and is too easy on people with higher incomes. We have progressive rates of taxation to take account of this; similarly, what you do for the poor should take an increasing percentage of your income as your income grows. Nevertheless, this is not a leveling-down exercise. We should retain incentives for people to work hard, take risks, and be innovative. Those with more can give more, but they will still be left with more.

Let's look at the incomes of America's superrich, rich, and merely comfortable, and ask what could reasonably be sought from them as a contribution toward meeting the problem of extreme poverty. Here's a first sketch of a public standard of acceptable giving.[12]

Start with the superrich. The top 0.01 percent of U.S. taxpayers have annual incomes above $10.7 million, and an average income of $29.6 million. At that level, giving away a third of their income would be unlikely to reduce their standard of living to any significant degree. The rest of the top 0.1 percent have an average income of nearly $3.7 million and a minimum income of $1.9 million. Let's put them down for a quarter of their income. The remainder of the top 0.5 percent have an average income of $955,000 and a minimum income of $600,000. They could give one fifth of what they earn.

Now we are moving down to income levels that make people rich, but not superrich. Those in the top 1 percent, but not the top 0.5 percent, earn a minimum income of $383,000 and an average income of $465,000. They could comfortably afford to give 15 percent of their income. Next, those in the top 5 percent, but not the top 1 percent, earn an average income of $210,000 annually, with a minimum income of $148,000. At this income level, the tithe—10 percent of one's income—can hardly be too demanding, since it has traditionally been given by people on far more modest incomes.

Completing the top 10 percent, and taking us to a level of income that, at least in the United States, is considered comfortable rather than rich, we have taxpayers earning an average income of $122,000 and a minimum income of $105,000. From them let's ask only a modest 5 percent.

That seems a tolerably fair level of donating from the highest-income 10 percent of American taxpayers to projects aimed at saving the lives and reducing the suffering of the world's poorest people. Some other sliding scale might arguably be as fair or fairer. Even if this scheme does no more than start a discussion, it will have served its purpose.

One question to consider is whether the scale should be based on gross or after-tax income. If the donations are fully tax-deductible, they should be based on gross income, because they will in any case reduce the amount of tax paid. But in some countries—Sweden is an example—donations are not tax-deductible. Then the scale should be based on after-tax income.

When I published a similar proposal in *The New York Times* in 2006, a Sacramento woman wrote that she and her husband were in the top 10 percent but "we have very little left at the end of each month. I can't remember the last time we went out to dinner, or a movie or anything like that . . . we didn't even go on a honeymoon!" Paying off student loans was one of their major expenses. It's true that an income that is more than adequate for people in some circumstances might leave much less discretionary income for those who have to pay back loans or put aside some money to ensure that their children can get a decent education. Much depends on whether people own their own home, and if so, whether they have a mortgage and how much the payments are. Taking these comments into account, I have modified the scheme I proposed in 2006, when I suggested that all those in the top 10 percent, but not the top 1 percent, give 10 percent of their income. Now I am proposing that those in the lower part of this group, that is, in the top 10 percent, but not in the top 5 percent, should give only 5 percent of their income.

The scale proposed above needed some fine-tuning, however, to avoid the creation of a penalty for moving from one income bracket into the next. For simplicity, I suggested that all income should be taxed at one rate, with that rate depending on the income bracket. So people whose income is $147,000 would, in my scheme, be giving away 5 percent, or $7,350, leaving themselves $139,650, but if their income rose to $148,000 they give away 10 percent, leaving only $133,200. That makes no sense. We can fix this problem in the same way as is done for progressive tax scales.

Income Bracket	Donation
$105,001–$148,000	5%
$148,001–$383,000	5% of the first $148,000 and 10% of the remainder
$383,001–$600,000	5% of the first $148,000, 10% of the next $235,000, and 15% of the remainder
$600,001–$1.9 million	5% of the first $148,000, 10% of the next $235,000, 15% of the next $217,000 and 20% of the remainder
$1,900,001–$10.7 million	5% of the first $148,000, 10% of the next $235,000, 15% of the next $217,000, 20% of the next $1.3 million, and 25% of the remainder
Over $10.7 million	5% of the first $148,000, 10% of the next $235,000, 15% of the next $217,000, 20% of the next $1.3 million, 25% of the next $8.8 million, and 33.33% of the remainder

Now let's add in the number of taxpayers in each bracket. With that information, and the average income in each bracket, we

can calculate how much the suggested levels of giving would
yield from American taxpayers.

Income Bracket	Number of Taxpayers	Average Income	Minimum Remaining	Total Raised
$105,001–$148,000	7,418,050	$122,353	$99,800	$45 billion
$148,001–$383,000	5,934,440	$210,325	$140,600	$81 billion
$383,001–$600,000	741,805	$464,716	$352,100	$32 billion
$600,001–$1.9 million	593,444	$955,444	$536,700	$80 billion
$1,900,001–$10.7 million	133,525	$3.7 million	$1.59 million	$102 billion
Over $10.7 million	14,836	$29.6 million	$8.19 million	$131 billion
Total	**14,836,100**			**$471 billion**

So these suggested levels of giving would yield a total of $471
billion a year for the world's poorest billion people—not from
all the world's affluent people, but from just 10 percent of
American families! (Sachs, remember, estimated that it would
take a maximum of $189 billion a year to meet the Millen-
nium Development Goals.)

Bill Clinton, in his bestselling book *Giving,* tells his readers
about the suggestions I made in my earlier *New York Times*
essay but then adds:

> I think it's unrealistic to expect this level of giving to
> global causes in the short run, for several reasons: some
> wealthy people don't believe the money will be spent
> wisely . . . some people with high incomes but little accu-
> mulated wealth want to build an estate before they give a
> large portion of their money away; $132,000 a year goes
> a lot further in Little Rock than it does in New York
> City; and many wealthy people are already committed to
> giving money to other charitable causes in America.[13]

Clinton goes on to suggest a more modest scheme, in which
those in the top 1 percent give 5 percent of their income, and
the rest of the top 10 percent give just 1 percent. For those in

the top 10 percent but not the top 1 percent, that is only one-third of what they already give, and would require nothing more than redirecting a portion of that giving from domestic charities to those working in the world's poorest countries.[14]

But is it really asking too much of people earning at least $383,000 to live on a pretax income of $352,100 instead? What is considered an "unrealistic" level of giving in one time and place may seem quite modest in another. Surprisingly, Americans earning less than $20,000 a year actually give a higher percentage of their income—a substantial 4.6 percent—to charity than every other income group until we get to those earning more than $300,000 a year.[15] That suggests that if the rich had the same culture of giving as the poor, they would give more than Clinton proposes. As we saw in chapter 5, much will depend on the way in which we appeal to people, and on the in-stitutional structures and social practices under which we live. Until we have tried to change these structures and practices as that chapter described, we cannot really know how much people may eventually be willing to give. It isn't clear exactly who Clinton has in mind when he refers to "wealthy people." But on the proportions of income I am recommending, those earning over, say, $300,000 a year will be able to meet the public stan-dard of contribution to the task of eliminating global poverty without coming remotely near impoverishing themselves. They will still be able to live at a very comfortable level, dine at good restaurants, go to concerts, take luxurious vacations, and change their wardrobes each season. I very much doubt that any of them will be noticeably less happy.

If your income doesn't put you in the top 10 percent, you still almost certainly have income that you can spare—remember that bottle of water or can of soda you bought in-stead of drinking the water that runs out of the tap? I won't specify the details, because as the letter from the Sacramento woman indicates, the percentage of a person's income available for discretionary spending varies greatly once their income gets down to around $100,000. But think about how much you can give. Getting to 5 percent may not be difficult, and will enable you to feel that you've done more than your share. And if the lower 90 percent of taxpayers were to give, on average, just 1 percent of their earnings, that, added to the suggested donations from the top 10 percent, would bring the total to around $510 billion.

Obviously, the rich in other nations should share the burden of relieving global poverty. There is an increasingly large number of wealthy people in non-OECD countries like China, India, Brazil, Chile, and South Africa. Of the 855 million rich people in the world, 17 percent, or 148 million, live in countries with average incomes below that of Portugal (and this figure is growing rapidly). This includes 11 percent who live in countries with average incomes below that of Brazil. These people should also be doing their share of combating global poverty, whether in their own countries or elsewhere.[16]

For simplicity, let's take one-third as a fair share for the United States, since that is roughly proportionate to the U.S. share of the total income of the OECD nations.[17] On that basis, extending the scheme I have suggested worldwide would provide more than $1.5 trillion annually for development aid. That's eight times what the UN task force estimated would be required to meet the Millennium Development Goals by 2015, and twenty times the shortfall between that sum and existing official development aid commitments.[18] It is ample to cover not only the aid itself, but also research and experimentation into what forms of aid work best.

It was not until I calculated how much America's richest 10 percent actually earn and compared that with what Sachs estimates would be required to meet the Millennium Development Goals that I fully understood how easy it would be for the world's rich to meet the basic needs of those living in extreme poverty all over the world. I found the result astonishing. I double-checked the figures and asked a research assistant to check them as well. But they were correct. If the UN task force is right, then the Millennium Development Goals are far too modest. If we fail to achieve them—as present indications say that we well may—we cannot excuse ourselves by saying that the target was a burdensome one, for it plainly is not. The target we should be setting for ourselves is not halving the proportion of people living in extreme poverty, and without enough to eat, but ensuring that no one needs to live permanently in such degrading conditions.

That goal is possible. Here's a seven-point plan that will make you part of the solution to world poverty.

1. Visit www.TheLifeYouCanSave.com and pledge to meet the standard.

2. Check out some of the links on the website, or do your own research, and decide to which organization or organizations you will give.

3. Take your income from your last tax return, and work out how much the standard requires you to give. Decide how you want to give it—in regular monthly installments, quarterly, or just once a year, whatever suits you best. Then do it!

4. Tell others what you have done. Spread the word in any way you can: talk, text, e-mail, blog, use whatever online connections you have. Try to avoid being self-righteous or preachy, because you're probably no saint, either, but let people know that they, too, can be part of the solution.

5. If you are employed by a corporation or institution, ask it to consider giving its employees a nudge in the right direction by setting up a scheme that will, unless they

choose to opt out, donate 1 percent of their pretax earnings to a charity helping the world's poorest people. (See chapter 5 for examples of such schemes.)

6. Contact your national political representatives and tell them you want your country's foreign aid to be directed only to the world's poorest people.

7. Now you've made a difference to some people living in extreme poverty. (Even if you can't see them or know whom you have helped.) Plus, you've demonstrated that human beings can be moved by moral argument. Feel good about being part of the solution.

The Greatest Motivation

If you and other well-off people in affluent nations were all to give, say, 5 percent of your income for the fight against global poverty, it would probably not reduce your happiness at all. You may have to make some adjustments to your spending, but quite possibly you will find that some of those adjustments make no difference to your well-being. Instead of having to spend money to keep up appearances because otherwise people will think you can't afford to buy new clothes or a new car, or to renovate your home, you now have a good reason for keeping the things that you find perfectly comfortable and serviceable: You have a better use for the money. And you could even end up happier, because taking part in a collective effort to help the world's poorest people would give your life greater meaning and fulfillment. As we have seen, people at Bear Stearns found their giving gratifying, and many members of the 50% League, including some who are by no means rich, feel that their giving has brought meaning and purpose to their lives. It can do the same for you.

Not long ago, at a dinner with the president of a university where I had given a talk, I found myself seated next to Carol Koller, a fund-raiser for the university. We began talking about giving and the role it plays in filling people's lives with meaning, and she told me the following story:

Soon after I began a new position as executive director of a medical center foundation, a board member told me about someone I should meet. He added that this person tended to be gruff, and rarely gave when asked. I was not in a hurry to meet him, but the medical center was preparing to build a clinic for low-income women and children, and he owned the land where they wanted to build. I was expected to get the land donated.

I made the call, introduced myself, and said there was a piece of land he owned that I would like to discuss. He responded that he would talk but that he was promising nothing. He chose my office for the meeting.

He arrived. He was a big man, intent on business and clearly accustomed to being in control. My office was small. We sat knee to knee. I explained the project. I asked that he work with me to figure out how to accomplish the task. To my amazement, his eyes began to fill with tears. He told me that everyone knew he could accomplish anything he attempted in business, but he had always wanted to do something of real value. He said that he did not know how and had not been able, until today, to find anyone who could help him.

He explained that people insulted him by asking for $5,000 or $10,000. He would send them away, often yelling at them to get out of his sight. Before leaving my office that day, he pledged $500,000.

I had not asked him for money at all. I had only asked him to work with me. This man had been waiting for years for someone to give him the chance to make the gift he had been longing to make. Before he died he had the joy of giving another $14 million to the community. At the dedication of another project he funded, in front of several hundred people, tears came to him again as he said, "There is a lady in the audience who changed my life."

For millennia, wise people have said that doing good brings fulfillment. Buddha advised his followers: "Set your heart on doing good. Do it over and over again, and you will be filled with joy." Socrates and Plato taught that the just man is happy.[19] Epicurus did, too. (Today we associate an "epicurean" with one who takes pleasure in fine food and wines. The philosopher who gave his name to that way of living, however, wrote: "It is impossible to live the pleasant life without also living sensibly, nobly and justly."[20])

The wisdom of the ancients still holds. A survey of 30,000 American households found that those who gave to charity were 43 percent more likely to say that they were "very happy" about their lives than those who did not give, and the figure was very similar for those who did voluntary work for charities as compared with those who did not. A separate study showed that those who give are 68 percent less likely to have felt "hopeless" and 34 percent less likely to say that they felt "so sad that nothing could cheer them up."[21]

The American Red Cross, which has vast experience with volunteer workers and blood donors, takes a similar view. It encourages people to volunteer by telling them: "Helping others feels good and helps you feel good about yourself." Jane Piliavin, a psychologist, put this to the test and found that giving blood does, like volunteering in general, make people feel good about themselves. The effect is particularly marked in older people—so marked, in fact, that there is even evidence that volunteering improves the health of elderly people and helps them live longer. Receiving assistance, on the other hand, doesn't have as great a beneficial impact. As psychologist Jonathan Haidt, author of *The Happiness Hypothesis,* comments, "At least for older people, it really is more blessed to give than to receive."[22]

The link between giving and happiness is clear, but surveys cannot show the direction of causation. Researchers have, however, looked at what happens in people's brains when they do good things. In one experiment, economists William Harbaugh and Daniel Burghart and psychologist Ulrich Mayr gave $100 to each of nineteen female students. While undergoing magnetic resonance imaging, which shows activity in various parts of the brain, the students were given the option of donating some of the money to a local food bank for the poor. To ensure that any effects observed came entirely from making the donation, and not, for instance, from having the belief that others would think they were generous people, the students were informed that no one, not even the experimenters, would know which students made a donation. The research found that when students donated, the brain's "reward centers"—the caudate nucleus, nucleus accumbens, and insulae—became active. These are the parts of the brain that respond when you eat something sweet or receive money. Altruists often talk of the "warm glow" they get from helping others. Now we have seen it happening in the brain.[23]

. . .

Most of us prefer harmony to discord, whether between ourselves and others or within our own minds. That inner harmony is threatened by any glaring discrepancy between the way you live and the way you think you ought to live. Your reasoning may tell you that you ought to be doing something substantial to help the world's poorest people, but your emotions may not move you to act in accordance with this view. If you are persuaded by the moral argument, but are not sufficiently motivated to act accordingly, I recommend that instead of worrying about how much you would have to do in order to live a fully ethical life, you do something that is significantly more than you have been doing so far. Then see how that feels. You may find it more rewarding than you imagined possible.

I was lucky enough to know Henry Spira, a man who spent his life campaigning for the downtrodden, the poor, and the oppressed. Since he never had much money, his form of philanthropy was to give his time, energy, and intelligence to making a difference. In the 1950s, he marched in the civil rights movement in the South. Sailing around the world as a merchant seaman, he worked for a rebel union organization fighting corrupt union bosses. The 1960s saw him teaching in some of New York City's toughest public high schools. In the 1970s, he became an extraordinarily effective advocate for animals; among his many achievements was persuading cosmetics companies to find alternatives to testing their products on animals.[24] When he was around seventy, Spira developed cancer and knew he did not have long to live. I spent a lot of time with him then, and in one of our conversations I asked him what had driven him to spend his life working for others. He replied:

> I guess basically one wants to feel that one's life has amounted to more than just consuming products and generating garbage. I think that one likes to look back and say that one's done the best one can to make this a better place for others. You can look at it from this point of view: What greater motivation can there be than doing whatever one possibly can to reduce pain and suffering?

Afterword

In the year since I sent the typescript of this book to press, two very significant events have occurred. One received immense publicity, and the other almost none.

The tragic earthquake that struck Haiti in January 2010 killed more than 200,000 people—some estimates say the toll could be as high as 300,000—and destroyed the homes of millions more. Television footage of the dazed and grieving survivors and of rescuers hauling people out of the rubble of collapsed buildings dominated news services for several days and elicited a huge wave of public sympathy. Approximately half a billion dollars was donated to relief efforts—not as much as was given after the 2004 Asian tsunami, or after Hurricane Katrina struck New Orleans, but still a very large sum for a disaster in a poor country, especially considering that the global economy was making a faltering recovery from the financial crisis that struck in 2007. In the United States more than 3 million Americans donated $10 each by texting "Haiti" to a phone number. Billionaire golfer Tiger Woods reportedly gave $3 million. In Rwanda, a group of community health workers making less than $200 a month raised $7000 for Haiti.

Many people took this response to the tragedy as an encouraging sign of the world's compassion for those in need. Yes, it is . . . but a sign of an only modest level of compassion. Three million people amount to just one percent of the population of the United States, and $10 is less than the cost of a movie ticket. What the Rwandan health workers did was much more impressive.

There was far less media coverage of the announcement in

September 2009 by UNICEF, the United Nations Children's Fund, that the number of children dying from poverty-related causes is continuing to fall. As described in this book, in 1960 that number was estimated at 20 million. By 2007 it had fallen below 10 million. That is a remarkable achievement, given that in 1960 the world's population was only 2.5 billion and by 2007 it had grown to 6.5 billion. Now, in the most recent available estimates, the annual number of children dying from poverty before their fifth birthday is 8.8 million. Hence the figure that I use in this book of 27,000 children dying every day should be reduced to 24,000. Saving 3,000 lives a day means that in 100 days, as many lives are saved as were lost in the Haitian tragedy. If we focus on the 24,000 lives lost we will of course feel dismay about the avoidable tragedy of so many children dying. Yet if we think about the progress made in just the last two years, we could greet the UNICEF data with rejoicing.

Because news based on statistics rather than on actual people does not get much media coverage, the myth that aid does not work still survives. This book has now been published in a dozen different countries, from Australia to Sweden and from Korea to Brazil, and I have done interviews about it and spoken to audiences around the world. Still the most common response to my argument continues to be that we are not under an obligation to give to the poor because if we do, most of what we give will not reach those who need it. The lack of attention given to the UNICEF data makes it difficult to inform the public that we are making progress and that aid, especially aid directed to improving the health of children, is a big part of that progress.

Ironically, given that so many people doubt the effectiveness of aid, aid targeted at saving the lives of children living in poverty is likely to be more cost-effective than emergency relief. Although emergency relief after natural disasters is certainly needed, in the chaos that prevails after a large natural disaster it is often unclear how much is needed, how it will reach the people who need it, and who will coordinate relief efforts. Longer-term aid, like making sure that there is greater preparedness for natural disasters (which, in an earthquake zone, includes rebuilding to a standard that will better withstand earthquakes) is likely to be a more effective use of our resources than pouring money in to help the victims afterwards.

The 8.8 million children who die from poverty each year are dispersed in villages and urban slums all over the world and there are no television cameras focused on them. It is more difficult to focus on the children who did *not* die but would have if there had been no aid-funded program to immunize them against measles, to bring them sanitation and safe water, to provide them with bednets against malaria, or to establish rural health clinics that can educate their parents on how to treat diarrhea.

Imagine that a million children are trapped by rising floodwaters on some high ground that is shrinking as the water continues to rise. We know that if we do not rescue them soon, they will die. Every news service would lead with the progress being made by the rescue efforts, there would be helicopters with television crews buzzing over their heads, and the networks would give the children 24-hour coverage. Our leaders would pledge to help them and we would all give generously until we knew that they were safe. Instead of this, the deaths of children in poor countries from diarrhea, measles, and malaria have become part of the background of the world we live in, and if we know about it at all, we are likely to believe that it is a problem that will always be with us. But that isn't so. In the last two years, we have saved a million children. In the coming years, if we all give substantially more, we can save the entire 8.8 million.

. . .

I am often asked if I am happy with the response to this book; but how could I be happy with it, as long as aid from the rich of the world to those in extreme poverty remains at its present very modest levels?

The point of writing the book was not to get good reviews in the newspapers, or even to sell a lot of copies. The point was, and remains, to bring about change in how we live. The most pleasing responses are always from people who have done something positive because they have read the book, or heard about what it argues. Fortunately many people have told me—in reviews, newspaper articles, emails, and when they have come up to me after a talk—that the book has changed how much they give. And thousands have gone to www.thelifeyoucansave.com and pledged to give in accordance with the standards set out in the final chapter of this book, and more are pledging all the time.

You can see many of the comments from people who have pledged, and photos of the people making the comments, on that website. Here are just a few examples:

> I have a purpose in life, which is way more important than all the Porsches, margaritas, and flat-screen TVs. I would be ashamed not to give. —Yevgenijs Veinbergs

> I am on an income of only £19,300, but I'm now making charitable donations of about 5% of this, as a result of *The Life You Can Save.* —Peter Bond

> I decided to pledge because I wanted to be a tiny part of demonstrating a shared understanding of how we should help extremely poor people. —Kathryn Smith

> I read Peter as a freshman in college. It helped me visualize my feelings and changed my direction in life. —Doug Bishop (who sent a photo of himself teaching school children in Ghana)

The ethical argument was just too compelling. —Nancy
Kosinski

We were inspired to pledge after reading Peter's book, as
there is simply no logical reason not to. —Charles
Gillanders and Anna Visser

Thank you for setting this [website] up; it helps me to
remember how trivial my problems are in the greater
scheme of things and how lucky I am. —Amanda
Catching

It is my 'atheist tithe' towards the eradication of suffering related to poverty. —Erroll Treslan (who also donated a copy of this book to every member of the
Canadian parliament)

I don't have much to spare, financially. Now that I know
how easy it is even for someone like me to save a life,
however, I've never thought twice about giving what I
can. —Cassandra Ingles

These, and many others too numerous to quote, are heart-
warming evidence of the human capacity to respond to an ethical argument. But I have two special favorites. One is from
Hugh Carnegy, the executive editor of the *Financial Times*.
One might have thought that he would have already known all
that there was to know about world poverty. Nevertheless, in
reviewing the book for his paper, he described the argument in
the final chapter of this book for a sliding scale of giving and
concluded with these words:

Faced with this argument, it is hard not to ask yourself
how your own giving measures up. Yes, I will go on buy-

ing things I do not really need. But, yes, this book has persuaded me that I should give more—significantly more—to help those less fortunate.

My very favorite response brings us back to the first chapter of this book, in which I asked you if you would rescue a child drowning in a shallow pond, even if doing so would ruin your new shoes. Christa Rogers sent the website a photo of herself with her family. She is wearing a fashionable pair of shoes. Her message said:

> I pledged because I could relate so directly to the opening illustration of saving a child at the cost of a pair of shoes. Until recently I was a member of a service that sent me a new pair of designer shoes every month, yet I was not giving anything to end poverty or help those in need. I cancelled that service and am now giving this money to the poor.

You can join Hugh Carnegy, Christa Rogers, and thousands of others from dozens of different countries by going to www.thelifeyoucansave.com and pledging to meet the guidelines for giving according to your income. Lend this book to others, encouraging them to read it and to sign the special pledge page found at the front of the book. If you run out of space, you can find a copy of the page on the website to print and circulate with the book. Your own pledge can make an important difference to a child, a family, even a village; but if the world is to change, the message needs to spread until the number who have pledged becomes a critical mass, changing attitudes in the affluent world so that we come to see helping those in great need as an indispensable part of what it is to live an ethical life.

Peter Singer
June 2010

Acknowledgments

An invitation from Professor Julian Savulescu to give the 2007 Uehiro Lectures in Practical Ethics at Oxford University got me started on this book. This annual lecture series is intended to show how major issues of the day can be discussed in a manner that is of a high academic standard, yet accessible to the general public. The lectures are funded by the Uehiro Foundation on Ethics and Education, chaired by Mr. Eiji Uehiro, and hosted by the Oxford Uehiro Centre for Practical Ethics. It was an honor to give the Uehiro Lectures for 2007, and I gratefully acknowledge the support of the Uehiro Foundation on Ethics and Education for enabling me to do so.

Another invitation, this time from Ilena Silverman of *The New York Times Sunday Magazine,* prodded me to put my views in a form that could reach a wide audience. Kathy Robbins, my literary agent, helped me find the right publisher. I couldn't have wished for a better editor than Tim Bartlett, who put an extraordinary amount of time and effort into showing me, again and again, how the next draft could convey my ideas more effectively than the one I had just given him. His assistant, Lindsey Schwoeri, was always helpful, and the support and encouragement from everyone at Random House has been wonderful.

In addition to the Uehiro Lectures, I have presented work related to this book to my colleagues and to the 2007–08 visiting fellows at the Center for Human Values at Princeton University, and—limiting myself to relatively more recent occasions—at: Scripps College; the University of California,

Los Angeles; Pacific Lutheran University; Quinnipiac University; Denison University; the Ethics Research Institute of the University of Zurich; the American Philosophical Society in Philadelphia; the University of Melbourne; Monash University; as one of my Dasan Lectures in Korea; and at the University of Stockholm, where I gave the 2008 Wedberg Lectures.

I particularly thank the following individuals, from whom I have received valued suggestions or information: Mallika Ahluwalia, Kwame Anthony Appiah, Steve Barney, Lyn Bender, Tyler Cowen, Rachel Croson, Pam DiLorenzo, Chris and Anne Ellinger, Eric Gregory, Jonathan Haidt, Elie Hassenfeld, James Hong, Dale Jamieson, Stanley Katz, Holden Karnofsky, Magda King, Carol Koller, Zell Kravinsky, Katarzyna de Lazari-Radek, David Morawetz, Chris Olivola, Jung Soon Park, Miyun Park, Toby Ord, Rebecca Ratner, Robert Reich, Geoff Russell, Agata Sagan, Pranay Sanklecha, Eldar Shafir, Jen Shang, Israel Shenker, Renata Singer, Paul Slovic, Louise Story, John Warnick, and Leif Wenar. Thanks, too, to the commentators on my Wedberg Lectures: Torbjörn Tännsjö, Folke Tersman, Eva Asplund, and Gustaf Arrhenius. In addition, as the text indicates, I have benefited for many years from the comments of my students in many courses in which we have discussed the issues covered in this book.

Michael Liffman, of the Asia-Pacific Centre for Philanthropy and Social Investment at Swinburne University, encouraged me to think about ethical issues specific to philanthropy, and cosponsored a conference at Princeton University on that topic. At Columbia University, Akeel Bilgrami brought me together with Joe Stiglitz and Bill Easterly in a stimulating discussion of the efficacy of aid. Moises Naim, of *Foreign Policy* arranged another lively debate for me, this time with Martin Wolf, in Monterrey, Mexico. At Oxfam America, Philip Weiser and Paul O'Brien kindly responded to my queries; and Aida Pesquera, from the Oxfam office in Bogotá, accompanied me on a visit to an Oxfam project in Colombia. Oxfam Australia arranged my visit to the ragpickers they were aiding in Pune, India, and Margie Bryant of Serendipity Productions, funded the trip as part of her documentary on my work. Howard Gardner put me in touch with Scott Seider, who allowed me to draw extensively from his then-unpublished research. Brent Howard provided extensive and astute research assistance, and Jessica Lucas helped with the calculations in chapter 10. At Princeton, Kim Girman has continued to assist in innumerable ways.

Above all, however, what I think about our obligations to the poor is the product of taking decisions together with Renata, my wife, to such an extent that I cannot say what I would be thinking, or doing, regarding these issues, had we not been together these past forty years.

Notes

Preface

1. Cara Buckley, "Man Is Rescued by Stranger on Subway Tracks," *The New York Times,* January 3, 2007.

2. Donald McNeil, "Child Mortality at Record Low: Further Drop Seen," *The New York Times,* September 13, 2007.

3. Kristi Heim, "Bulk of Buffett's Fortune Goes to Gates Foundation," *The Seattle Times,* June 26, 2006.

1. Saving a Child

1. BBC News, September 21, 2007, http://news.bbc.co.uk/2/hi/ uk_news/england/manchester/7006412.stm.

2. Deepa Narayan with Raj Patel, Kai Schafft, Anne Rademacher, and Sarah Koch-Schulte. *Voices of the Poor: Can Anyone Hear Us?* Published for the World Bank by Oxford University Press (New York, 2000), p. 36.

3. This is a compilation of things said by the poor, cited in ibid., p. 28.

4. World Bank Press Release, "New Data Show 1.4 Billion Live on Less Than US$1.25 a Day, But Progress Against Poverty Remains Strong," August 26, 2008, http://go.worldbank.org/ T0TEVOV4E0. The estimate is based on price data from 2005, and does not reflect increases in food prices in 2008, which are likely to have increased the number below the poverty line. For the research on which the press release is based, see Shaohua Chen and Martin Ravallion, "The Developing World Is Poorer Than We Thought, But No Less Successful in the Fight Against Poverty," Policy Research Working Paper 4073, World Bank

Development Research Group, August 2008, www-wds.worldbank
.org/external/default/WDSContentServer/IW3P/IB/2008/08/26/
000158349_20080826113239/Rendered/PDF/WPS4703.pdf.

For further discussion of World Bank statistics, see Sanjay
Reddy and Thomas Pogge, "How *Not* to Count the Poor,"
www.columbia.edu/~sr793/count.pdf, and Martin Ravallion,
"How *Not* to Count the Poor: A Reply to Reddy and Pogge,"
www.columbia.edu/~sr793/wbreply.pdf.

5. Robert Rector and Kirk Anderson, "Understanding Poverty in
America," Heritage Foundation Backgrounder #1713 (2004),
www.heritage.org/Research/Welfare/bg1713.cfm. Rector and
Anderson draw on data available from the 2003 U.S. Census
Bureau report on poverty and on various other government
reports.

6. United Nations, Office of the High Representative for the Least
Developed Countries, Landlocked Developing Countries and the
Small Island Developing States, and World Bank, World Bank
Development Data Group, "Measuring Progress in Least
Developed Countries: A Statistical Profile" (2006), tables 2 and 3,
pp. 14–15. Available at www.un.org/ohrlls/.

7. United Nations Development Program, *Human Development
Report 2000* (Oxford University Press, New York, 2000) p. 30;
Human Development Report 2001 (Oxford University Press, New
York, 2001) pp. 9–12, p. 22; and World Bank, *World Development
Report 2000/2001,* overview, p. 3, www.worldbank.org/poverty/
wdrpoverty/report/overview.pdf, for the other figures. The
Human Development Reports are available at http://hdr.undp.org.

8. James Riley, *Rising Life Expectancy: A Global History* (New York:
Cambridge University Press, 2001); Jeremy Laurance, "Thirty
Years: Difference in Life Expectancy Between the World's Rich
and Poor Peoples," *The Independent* (UK), September 7, 2007.

9. "Billionaires 2008," *Forbes,* March 24, 2008, www.forbes
.com/forbes/2008/0324/080.html.

10. Joe Sharkey, "For the Super-Rich, It's Time to Upgrade the Old
Jumbo," *The New York Times,* October 17, 2006.

11. "Watch Your Time," Special Advertising Supplement to *The New
York Times,* October 14, 2007. The passage quoted is on p. 40.

12. Bill Marsh, "A Battle Between the Bottle and the Faucet," *The New York Times,* July 15, 2007.

13. Pacific Institute, "Bottled Water and Energy: A Fact Sheet," www.pacinst.org/topics/water_and_sustainability/bottled _water/bottled_water_and_energy.html.

14. Lance Gay, "Food Waste Costing Economy $100 Billion, Study Finds," Scripps Howard News Service, August 10, 2005, www.knoxstudio.com/shns/story.cfm?pk=GARBAGE-08-10-05.

15. Deborah Lindquist, "How to Look Good Naked," Lifetime Network, Season 2, Episode 2, July 29, 2009. As relayed by Courtney Moran.

2. *Is It Wrong Not to Help?*

1. Peter Unger, *Living High and Letting Die* (New York: Oxford University Press, 1996).

2. For further discussion see Peter Singer, *The Expanding Circle,* (Oxford: Clarendon Press, 1981), pp. 136, 183. For futher examples, see www.unification.net/ws/theme015.htm.

3. Luke 18:22–25; Matthew 19:16–24.

4. Luke 10:33.

5. Luke 14:13.

6. Matthew 25:31–46.

7. Second Letter to the Corinthians, 8:14.

8. Acts 2:43–47; see also 4:32–37.

9. Thomas Aquinas, *Summa Theologica,* II-II, Question 66, Article 7.

10. John Locke, *Two Treatises of Government,* Book I, Paragraph 42.

11. Erin Curry, "Jim Wallis, Dems Favorite Evangelical?" *Baptist Press,* January 19, 2005, www.bpnews.net/bpnews.asp?ID=19941.

12. Nicholas Kristof, "Evangelicals a Liberal Can Love," *The New York Times,* February 3, 2008.

13. Babylonian Talmud, Bava Bathra 9a; Maimonides, Mishneh Torah, "Laws Concerning Gifts for the Poor," 7:5.

14. Mengzi [Mencius] Liang Hui Wang I, http://chinese.dsturgeon.net/text.pl?node=16028&if=en.

3. Common Objections to Giving

1. Center on Philanthropy at Indiana University, *Giving USA 2008: The Annual Report on Philanthropy for the Year 2007,* Glenview, IL: Giving USA Foundation, 2008, pp. 9, 48. The comparative figure covers the period 1995–2002, and is from the Comparative Nonprofit Sector Project at the Center for Civil Society Studies at the Johns Hopkins Institute of Policy Studies, Table 5, www.jhu.edu/~cnp/PDF/compatable5_dec05.pdf.

2. Eli Portillo and Sadie Latifi, "American Volunteer Rate a Steady 28.8%," *San Diego Union-Tribune,* June 13, 2006. The comparative data are again from the Comparative Nonprofit Sector Project.

3. *Giving USA 2008,* pp. 9–14, 40; Organisation for Economic Co-operation and Development (OECD), Statistical Annex of the 2007 Development Co-operation Report, www.oecd.org/dataoecd/52/9/1893143.xls, Table 7e. The "most optimistic" estimate for the percentage of religious giving that goes to foreign aid comes from the Hudson Institute's Index of Global Philanthropy, 2008. This suggests that religious institutions contribute $8.8 billion to foreign aid. It also gives a total figure for U.S. private philanthropy almost four times as high as the OECD figure. Some of the discrepancy can be explained by the broader scope of the Index of Global Philanthropy figures—which include, for example, time worked by volunteers, costed at average U.S. wage levels—but it nevertheless remains unclear how this figure can be reconciled with the OECD or the Giving USA data. See Center for Global Prosperity, Index of Global Philanthropy, Hudson Institute, 2008, available at http://gpr.hudson.org/.

4. Peter Singer, "The Singer Solution to World Poverty," *The New York Times Sunday Magazine,* September 5, 1999.

5. Glennview High School is Seider's fictional name for the school, and the names of the students are also pseudonyms. Material about Glennview High School students is drawn from Scott Seider, "Resisting Obligation: How Privileged Adolescents Conceive of Their Responsibilities to Others," *Journal of Research in Character Education,* 6:1 (2008), pp. 3–19, and Scott Seider,

Literature, Justice and Resistance: Engaging Adolescents from Privileged Groups in Social Action, unpublished doctoral dissertation, Graduate School of Education, Harvard University.

6. Jan Narveson, " 'We Don't Owe Them a Thing!' A Tough-minded but Soft-hearted View of Aid to the Faraway Needy," *The Monist,* 86:3 (2003), p. 419.

7. James B. Davies, Susanna Sandstrom, Anthony Shorrocks, and Edward N. Wolff, "The World Distribution of Household Wealth," Worldwide Institute for Development Economics Research of the United Nations University, Helsinki (December 2006), www.wider.unu.edu/research/2006-2007/2006-2007-1/wider-wdhw-launch-5-12-2006/wider-wdhw-report-5-12-2006.pdf.

8. Sharon Lafraniere, "Europe Takes Africa's Fish, and Boatloads of Migrants Follow," *The New York Times,* January 14, 2008, and Elizabeth Rosenthal, "Europe's Appetite for Seafood Propels Illegal Trade," *The New York Times,* January 15, 2008.

9. See Leif Wenar, "Property Rights and the Resource Curse," *Philosophy & Public Affairs* 36:1 (2008), pp. 2–32. A more detailed version is available on Wenar's website: www.wenar.staff.shef.ac.uk/PRRCwebpage.html.

10. Paul Collier, *The Bottom Billion* (New York: Oxford University Press, 2007).

11. See Leonard Wantchekon, "Why Do Resource Dependent Countries Have Authoritarian Governments?" *Journal of African Finance and Economic Development* 5:2 (2002), pp. 57–77; an earlier version is available at www.yale.edu/leitner/pdf/1999-11.pdf. See also Nathan Jensen and Leonard Wantchekon, "Resource Wealth and Political Regimes in Africa," *Comparative Political Studies,* 37 (2004), pp. 816–841.

12. President Museveni was speaking at the African Union summit, Addis Ababa, Ethiopia, February 2007, and the speech was reported in Andrew Revkin, "Poor Nations to Bear Brunt as World Warms," *The New York Times,* April 1, 2007.

13. Andrew Revkin, op. cit., and "Reports from Four Fronts in the War on Warming," *The New York Times,* April 3, 2007; Kathy

Marks, "Rising Tide of Global Warming Threatens Pacific Island States," *The Independent* (UK), October 25, 2006.

14. Organisation for Economic Co-operation and Development *(OECD), OECD Journal on Development: Development Co-operation Report 2007,* p. 134, www.oecd.org/dac/dcr. The table is reproduced by kind permission of OECD. See also *Statistical Annex of the 2007 Development Co-operation Report,* www.oecd.org/dataoecd/52/9/1893143.xls, Fig. 1e.

15. Program on International Policy Attitudes, www.worldpublicopinion.org/pipa/articles/home_page/383.php ?nid=&id=&pnt=383&lb=hmpg1. The table is reproduced by kind permission of the Program on International Policy Attitudes, and is taken from "Americans on Foreign Aid and World Hunger: A Survey of U.S. Public Attitudes" (February 2, 2001), http://65.109.167.118/pipa/pdf.feb01/ForeignAid_Feb01 _rpt.pdf.

16. Organisation for Economic Co-operation and Development (OECD), Statistical Annex of the 2007 Development Co-operation Report, www.oecd.org/dataoecd/52/9/1893143 .xls, Table 7e. If we accept the much higher estimate of U.S. private philanthropy in the Hudson Institute's Index of Global Philanthropy, America's total aid contribution rises to 0.42 percent, which is more respectable, although still slightly below the average country effort for official aid. The Index of Global Philanthropy figures are not suitable for international comparisons, however, as we lack figures calculated on a similar basis for most other countries.

17. See, for example, Anthony Langlois, "Charity and Justice in the Singer Solution," in Raymond Younis (ed) *On the Ethical Life* (Newcastle upon Tyne: Cambridge Scholars, forthcoming); Paul Gomberg, "The Fallacy of Philanthropy," *Canadian Journal of Philosophy* 32:1 (2002), pp. 29–66.

18. Gomberg, *op. cit.,* pp. 30, 63–64.

19. See Andy Lamey's response to Anthony Langlois's paper in the volume referred to in n. 17, above.

20. Claude Rosenberg and Tim Stone, "A New Take on Tithing," *Stanford Social Innovation Review,* Fall 2006, pp. 22–29.

21. Colin McGinn, as quoted by Michael Specter in "The Dangerous Philosopher," *The New Yorker,* September 6, 1999.

22. Alan Ryan, as quoted by Michael Specter in "The Dangerous Philosopher," *The New Yorker,* September 6, 1999.

23. http://www.muzakandpotatoes.com/2008/02/peter-singer-on -affluence.html.

4. Why Don't We Give More?

1. C. Daniel Batson and Elizabeth Thompson, "Why Don't Moral People Act Morally? Motivational Considerations," *Current Directions in Psychological Science* 10:2 (2001), pp. 54–57.

2. D. A. Small, G. Loewenstein, and P. Slovic, "Sympathy and Callousness: The Impact of Deliberative Thought on Donations to Identifiable and Statistical Victims," *Organizational Behavior and Human Decision Processes* 102 (2007), pp. 143–53; Paul Slovic, "If I Look at the Mass I Will Never Act: Psychic Numbing and Genocide," *Judgment and Decision Making* 2:2 (2007), pp. 79–95. I owe the references in this paragraph to this article. The research generally supports the claim made by Peter Unger in *Living High and Letting Die* (New York: Oxford University Press, 1996, pp. 28–29, 77–79), that our intuitions are distorted by a focus on a single identifiable victim, and in contrast we are prone to "futility thinking" in cases where we can, at best, save a few of many thousands of victims.

3. D. Västfjäll, E. Peters, and P. Slovic, "Representation, Affect, and Willingness-to-Donate to Children in Need." Unpublished manuscript in preparation.

4. See T. Kogut and I. Ritov, "An Identified Group, or Just a Single Individual?" *Journal of Behavioral Decision Making* 18 (2005), pp. 157–67; and T. Kogut and I. Ritov, "The Singularity of Identified Victims in Separate and Joint Evaluations," *Organizational Behavior and Human Decision Processes* 97 (2005), pp. 106–116.

5. Mark Babineck, "Jessica's Family Stays Low-key Ten Years After Water Well Drama," *Tex News,* October 14, 1997, www.texnews .com/texas97/jess101497.html; Mike Celizic, "Where Is Jessica McClure Now? *Today,* MSNBC, June 11, 2007, www.msnbc .msn.com/id/19104012/.

6. For discussion, see D. C. Hadorn, "The Oregon Priority-Setting Exercise: Cost-effectiveness and the Rule of Rescue, Revisited," *Medical Decision Making* 16 (1996), pp. 117–19; J. McKie and J. Richardson, "The Rule of Rescue," *Social Science and Medicine* 56 (2003), pp. 2407–19.

7. D. A. Small, and G. Loewenstein "Helping the Victim or Helping a Victim: Altruism and Identifiability," *Journal of Risk and Uncertainty,* 26:1 (2003), pp. 5–16.

8. Adapted from Paul Slovic, who has in turn adapted it from Seymour Epstein, "Integration of the Cognitive and the Psychodynamic Unconscious," *American Psychologist* 49 (1994), pp. 709–24. Slovic refers to the two systems as "experiential" and "analytic."

9. Quoted, but without further attribution, in Paul Slovic, "If I Look at the Mass I Will Never Act: Psychic Numbing and Genocide," *Judgment and Decision Making,* 2:2 (2007), pp. 79–95.

10. D. A. Small, G. Loewenstein, and P. Slovic, "Sympathy and Callousness: The Impact of Deliberative Thought on Donations to Identifiable and Statistical Victims," *Organizational Behavior and Human Decision Processes* 102 (2007), pp. 143–53.

11. Adam Smith, *Theory of the Moral Sentiments,* III.i.45.

12. Figures in this paragraph come from www.charitynavigator.com and from Steven Dubner, "How Pure Is Your Altruism?" *The New York Times,* May 13, 2008, http://freakonomics.blogs.nytimes .com/2008/05/13/how-pure-is-your-altruism/. Figures for the sums raised vary slightly between these two sources.

13. Since a man's biological investment in each child is far less than a woman's, and men can, in theory, have far more children, some fathers can succeed in passing on their genes without much concern for the welfare of each child. But a glance at human societies shows that this is the exception rather than the rule.

14. Charles Dickens, *Bleak House,* chapter 4; the relevant section is reprinted in Peter and Renata Singer, eds., *The Moral of the Story* (Oxford, UK: Blackwell, 2005), pp. 63–69.

15. Adam Smith, *Theory of the Moral Sentiments,* III.i.50.

16. D. Fetherstonhaugh, P. Slovic, S. M. Johnson, and J. Friedrich, "Insensitivity to the Value of Human Life: A Study of Psychophysical Numbing, *Journal of Risk and Uncertainty* 14 (1997), pp. 283–300. The roots of this research go back to work by Daniel Kahnemann and Amos Tversky. See Daniel Kahnemann and Amos Tversky, "Prospect Theory: An Analysis of Decision Under Risk," *Econometrica* 47 (1979), 263–91.

17. Paul Slovic, "If I Look at the Mass I Will Never Act: Psychic Numbing and Genocide," op. cit.

18. See Rachel Manning, Mark Levine, and Alan Collins, "The Kitty Genovese Murder and the Social Psychology of Helping," *American Psychologist* 62:6 (2007), pp. 555–62. I am grateful to Chrissy Holland for this reference.

19. Bib Latané and John Darley, *The Unresponsive Bystander* (New York: Appleton-Century-Crofts, 1970), p. 58. I am grateful to Judith Lichtenberg, "Famine, Affluence and Psychology," in Jeffrey Schaller, ed., *Peter Singer Under Fire* (Chicago: Open Court, forthcoming 2009) both for suggesting the relevance of this research and for this and other references.

20. Bib Latané and John Darley, *The Unresponsive Bystander,* chapters 6 and 7.

21. There is a substantial literature on the ultimatum game. For a useful discussion, see Martin Nowak, Karen Page, and Karl Sigmund, "Fairness Versus Reason in the Ultimatum Game," *Science* 289 (2000), pp. 1773–75.

22. S. F. Brosnan and F.B.M. de Waal, "Monkeys Reject Unequal Pay," *Nature* 425 (September 18, 2003), pp. 297–99.

23. Kathleen Vohs, Nicole Mead, and Miranda Goode, "The Psychological Consequences of Money," *Science* 314 (2006), pp. 1154–56.

24. Richard Titmuss, *The Gift Relationship: From Human Blood to Social Policy* (London: Allen & Unwin, 1970).

25. Elizabeth Corcoran, "Ruthless Philanthropy," www.Forbes.com, June 23, 2008.

26. For a fuller discussion of the relevance of our evolved psychology to ethics, see Peter Singer, *The Expanding Circle: Ethics and Sociobiology* (New York: Farrar, Straus & Giroux, 1981).

5. Creating a Culture of Giving

1. See Bib Latané and John Darley, "Group Inhibition of Bystander Intervention," *Journal of Personality and Social Psychology* 10 (1968), pp. 215–221; John Darley and Bib Latané, "Bystander Intervention in Emergencies: Diffusion of Responsibility," *Journal of Personality and Social Psychology* 8 (1968), pp. 377–83; Bib Latané and J. Rodin, "A Lady in Distress: Inhibiting Effects of Friends and Strangers on Bystander Intervention," *Journal of Experimental Social Psychology* 8 (1969), pp. 189–202; John Darley and Bib Latané, *The Unresponsive Bystander: Why Doesn't He Help?* (New York: Appleton-Century-Crofts, 1970).

2. Lee Ross and Richard E. Nisbett, *The Person and the Situation: Perspectives of Social Psychology* (Philadelphia: Temple University Press, 1991), especially pp. 27–46; Robert Cialdini, *Influence: Science and Practice* (4th ed. Boston: Allyn and Bacon, 2001). See also Judith Lichtenberg, "Absence and the Unfond Heart: Why People Are Less Giving Than They Might Be," in Deen Chatterjee, ed., *The Ethics of Assistance: Morality and the Distant Needy* (Cambridge, UK: Cambridge University Press, 2004).

3. Jen Shang and Rachel Croson, "Field Experiments in Charitable Contribution: The Impact of Social Influence on the Voluntary Provision of Public Goods," *The Economic Journal,* forthcoming. Renewing members gave 43 percent more when they were given the appropriate information, and new members 29 percent more. For the mail survey, see Rachel Croson and Jen Shang, "The Impact of Downward Social Information on Contribution Decision," *Experimental Economics* 11 (2008), pp. 221–33.

4. Matthew 6:1.

5. Charles Isherwood, "The Graffiti of the Philanthropic Class," *The New York Times,* December 2, 2007.

6. www.boldergiving.org.

7. Plan International, "Sponsor a Child: Frequently Asked Questions," www.plan-international.org/sponsorshipform/ sponsorfaq/, accessed January 16, 2008.

8. Eric Johnson and Daniel Goldstein, "Do Defaults Save Lives?" *Science* 302 (November 2003), pp. 1338–39. I owe this reference to Eldar Shafir, whose comments on this topic were very helpful.

9. Richard Thaler and Cass Sunstein, *Nudge: Improving Decisions about Health, Wealth and Happiness* (New Haven, CT: Yale University Press, 2008).

10. Brigitte Madrian and Dennis Shea, "The Power of Suggestion: Inertia in 401(k) Participation and Savings Behavior," *Quarterly Journal of Economics* 116:4 (2001), pp. 1149–87.

11. Louise Story, "A Big Salary With a Big Stipulation: Share It," *The New York Times,* November 12, 2007.

12. Katie Hafner, "Philanthropy Google's Way: Not the Usual," *The New York Times,* September 14, 2006; Harriet Rubin, "Google Offers a Map for Its Philanthropy," *The New York Times,* January 18, 2008.

13. Alexis de Tocqueville, *Democracy in America,* ed. J. P. Mayer, trans. G. Lawrence (Garden City, N.Y.: Anchor, 1969), p. 546. I owe the reference, and much else in this section, to Dale Miller, "The Norm of Self-interest," *American Psychologist* 54 (1999), pp. 1053–60. See also Dale Miller and Rebecca Ratner, "The Disparity Between the Actual and Assumed Power of Self-interest," *Journal of Personality and Social Psychology* 74 (1998), pp. 53–62, and Rebecca Ratner and Dale Miller, "The Norm of Self-interest and Its Effect on Social Action," *Journal of Personality and Social Psychology* 81 (2001), pp. 5–16.

14. David Thomas, "Anonymous Altruists," *The Telegraph* (UK) *Magazine,* October 27, 2007.

15. Dale Miller, "The Norm of Self-interest," *American Psychologist* 54 (1999), pp. 1053–60.

16. Robert Frank, T. Gilovich, and D. Regan, "Does Studying Economics Inhibit Cooperation?" *Journal of Economic Perspectives* 7 (1993), pp. 159–71.

17. Rebecca Ratner and Jennifer Clarke, "Negativity Conveyed to Social Actors Who Lack a Personal Connection to the Cause," unpublished manuscript.

18. Robert Wuthnow, *Acts of Compassion* (Princeton, N.J.: Princeton University Press, 1990), pp. 16, 72, 77.

6. How Much Does It Cost to Save a Life, and How Can You Tell Which Charities Do It Best?

1. David Koplow, *Smallpox: The Fight to Eliminate a Global Scourge* (Berkeley, CA: University of California Press, 2003).

2. Center for Global Development, "Millions Saved: Proven Successes in Global Health," 2007 edition, www.cgdev.org/doc/ millions/Millions_Saved_07.pdf, based on Ruth Levine and the What Works Working Group with Molly Kinder, *Millions Saved: Proven Successes in Global Health,* 2nd ed. (Boston: Jones and Bartlett, 2007).

3. Andrea Gerlin, "A Simple Solution," *Time,* October 8, 2006. See also the Rehydration Project, http://rehydrate.org/facts.

4. UNICEF, "Immunization Plus: The Big Picture," www.unicef .org/immunization/index_bigpicture.html.

5. www.nothingbutnets.net. Accessed June 12, 2008.

6. John Peabody, Mario Taguiwalo, David Robalino, and Julio Frenk, "Improving the Quality of Care in Developing Countries," in Dean Jamison et al., eds., *Disease Priorities in Developing Countries,* 2nd ed. (New York: Oxford University Press, 2006), p. 1304. Available online as part of Health Systems, a publication of the Disease Control Priorities Project, International Bank for Reconstruction and Development/The World Bank, files.dcp2.org/pdf/ expressbooks/healths.pdf.

7. William Easterly, *The White Man's Burden* (New York: The Penguin Press, 2006), p. 252.

8. www.interplast.org/programs.

9. Dean Karlan and Jonathan Zinman, "Expanding Credit Access:

Using Randomized Supply Decisions to Estimate the Impacts," Center for Economic Policy Research Discussion Paper DP 6180 (2007), available at www.cepr.org/pubs/dps/DP6180.asp.

10. GiveWell Research Report, "Global Poverty (Focus on Africa)," 2008, www.givewell.net/cause2.

11. This and other studies in this paragraph not separately referenced are taken from William Easterly, *The White Man's Burden*, pp. 372-75.

12. John Hilsenrath, "Economists Are Putting Theories to Scientific Test," *The Wall Street Journal*, December 28, 2006.

13. For further details see "India: Ragpickers Take Control," Oxfam News (Australia) September 2003, www.oxfam.org.au/oxfamnews/september_2003/india.html; Snehal Sonawane, "Rescuing Ragpickers," *The Times of India*, August 31, 2007, timesofindia.indiatimes.com/articleshow/2324932.cms.

14. Chris Hufstader, "Balancing Culture, New Law, in Mozambique," Oxfam America, February 24, 2006, www.oxfamamerica.org/whatwedo/where_we_work/southern_africa/news_publication/feature_story.2006-02-24.0346532995.

15. Oxfam International, "Mozambique's Family Law Passes!" www.oxfam.org/en/programs/development/safrica/moz_law.htm.

16. The figures are adjusted for inflation and converted from Australian dollars to 2007 U.S. dollars. I am grateful to Toby Ord for some of these calculations, and for drawing my attention to the Fred Hollows Foundation as an example of cost-effective aid. The Fred Hollows Foundation has been helpful in providing further information.

17. From interviews conducted by Mary Olive Smith and Amy Bucher, codirectors of *A Walk to Beautiful*, in April 2005 and November 2006, available through Nova online www.pbs.org/wgbh/nova/beautiful/hamlin.html.

18. UNFPA, the United Nations Population Fund, and EngenderHealth, "Obstetric Fistula Needs Asssessment Report: Findings from Nine African Countries" (2003), p. 4, www.unfpa.org/fistula.docs/fistular-needs-assessment.pdf.

19. www.worldwidefistulafund.org/Patient%20Care.html.

20. See also Lewis Wall, "Obstetric Vesicovaginal Fistula As an International Public-Health Problem," *The Lancet* 368 (September 30, 2006), 1201–1209.

21. T. Tengs, M. Adams, J. Pliskin, D. Safran, J. Siegel, M. Weinstein, and J. Graham, "Five Hundred Life-saving Interventions and Their Cost-effectiveness," *Risk Analysis* 15:3 (June 1995), pp. 369–90. The study found that the median cost per life-year saved was $42,000. In order to compare this figure with saving the life of a child with a life expectancy of fifty years, I have multiplied that figure by fifty.

22. David Fahrentholt, "Cosmic Markdown: EPA Says Life Is Worth Less," *The Washington Post,* July 19, 2008.

7. Improving Aid

1. William Easterly, *The White Man's Burden* (London: Penguin, 2007), p. 4.

2. See *OECD Statistical Annex of the 2007 Development Co-operation Report,* www.oecd.org/dataoecd/52/9/1893143.xls, Fig. 1e. The current level for all wealthy nations combined is 0.31 percent. In 1982–83, the level was 0.23 percent, and in 1993, 0.30 percent. See United Nations Human Development Report, 1995, p. 204, table 29, available at http://hdr.undp.org/en/media/hdr _1995_en_indicators2.pdf.

3. Organisation for Economic Co-operation and Development (OECD) Donor Aid Charts, www.oecd.org/countrylist/ 0,2578,en_2649_37413_1783495_1_1_1_37413,00.html; see also Oxfam America, "Smart Development: Why U.S. Foreign Aid Demands Major Reform," February 2008, www .oxfamamerica.org/newsandpublications/publications/briefing _papers/smart-development/smart-development-feb2008.pdf.

4. Branko Milanovic, *Worlds Apart: Measuring International and Global Inequality* (Princeton, N.J.: Princeton University Press, 2005), pp. 152–53, table 12.1; United Nations Human Development Report, 2007–2008, p. 289, Table 17, available

at http://hdr.undp.org/en/media/hdr_20072008_en
_indicator_tables.pdf.

5. Celia Dugger, "Kenyan Farmers' Fate Caught Up in U.S. Aid
Rules," *The New York Times,* July 31, 2007; Editorial, "A Surer
Way to Feed the Hungry," *The New York Times,* August 4, 2007;
Celia Dugger, "U.S. Jobs Shape Condoms' Role in Foreign Aid,"
The New York Times, October 29, 2006.

6. Celia Dugger, "CARE Turns Down Federal Funds for Food Aid,"
The New York Times, August 16, 2007; Daniel Maxwell and
Christopher Barrett, *Food Aid After Fifty Years: Recasting Its Role*
(London: Routledge, 2005), p. 35.

7. William Easterly, *The White Man's Burden* (London: Penguin,
2007), is among them. See also Raghuram Rajan and Arvind
Subramanian, "Aid and Growth: What Does the Cross-Country
Evidence Really Show?" IMF Working Paper 05/127
(Washington, D.C.: International Monetary Fund, 2005).

8. Martin Wolf, *Why Globalization Works* (New Haven, CT.: Yale
University Press, 2004).

9. See Organisation for Economic Co-operation and Development,
"Recipient Aid Charts," www.oecd.org/countrylist/0,3349,en
_2649_34469_25602317_1_1_1_1,00.html; for discussion see
Tim Harford and Michael Klein, "Aid and the Resource Curse,"
Public Policy for the Private Sector, Note 291, April 2005,
http://rru.worldbank.org/Documents/PublicPolicyJournal/
291Harford_Klein.pdf.

10. Raghuram Rajan and Arvind Subramanian, "What Undermines
Aid's Impact on Growth?" International Monetary Fund Working
Paper, WP/05/126, June 2005, www.imf.org/external/pubs/ft/wp/
2005/wp05126.pdf; Paul Collier, *The Bottom Billion,* (New York:
Oxford University Press, 2007), pp. 162–63.

11. Paolo de Renzio and Joseph Hanlon, "Contested Sovereignty in
Mozambique: The Dilemmas of Aid Dependence," Global
Economic Governance Working Paper 2007/25, January 2007,
www.globaleconomicgovernance.org/docs/Derenzio%20and
%20Hanlon_Mozambique%20paper%20rev%20120107.pdf.

12. UN Millennium Project, *Investing in Development: A Practical Plan to Achieve the Millennium Development Goals* (London: Earthscan, 2005), pp. 247–48, www.unmillennium project.org/reports.

13. "Reform of US Cotton Subsidies Could Feed, Educate Millions in Poor West African Countries," Oxfam Press Release, June 22, 2007, www.oxfam.org/node/173.

14. Kym Anderson and Alan Winters, "Subsidies and Trade Barriers: The Challenge of Reducing International Trade and Migration Barriers," Copenhagen Consensus 2008 Challenge Paper, www.copenhagenconsensus.com/Default.aspx?ID=1151; for some doubts about the possibility of measuring the gains, see the paper by Anthony Venables at the same location.

15. Sophia Murphy and Steve Suppan, "The 2008 Farm Bill and the Doha Agenda," Institute for Agriculture and Trade Policy, June 25, 2008, www.iatp.org/iatp/commentaries.cfm ?refID=103103; David Stout, "House Votes to Override Bush's Veto of Farm Bill," *The New York Times,* May 22, 2008.

16. CIA World Factbook, www.cia.gov/library/publications/ the-world-factbook/rankorder/2091rank.html. On the general question of the relationship between national income and human development indicators, see Jean Drèze and Amartya Sen, *Hunger and Public Action* (Oxford, UK: Clarendon Press, 1989).

17. Robert Guth, "Bill Gates Issues Call for Kinder Capitalism," *The Wall Street Journal,* January 24, 2008.

18. George W. Bush, quoted in "The Millennium Challenge Account," www.whitehouse.gov/infocus/developingnations/ millennium.html.

19. Paul Collier, *The Bottom Billion,* p. 106.

20. Ibid., p. 114.

21. Jeffrey Sachs, "Rapid Victories Against Extreme Poverty," *Scientific American* 296:4 (April 2007), p. 34, www.sciam.com/ article.cfm?articleID=5B978D32-E7F2-99DF -304C9630D4CE6254.

22. Jeffrey Sachs, *Common Wealth: Economics for a Crowded Planet*

(New York: Penguin, 2008), pp. 238–41; www.millennium villages.org.

23. "Millennium Villages: A New Approach to Fighting Poverty: FAQ," www.unmillenniumproject.org/mv/mv_faq.htm; "The Magnificent Seven," *The Economist,* April 26, 2006, p. 63.

24. Thomas Malthus, *An Essay on the Principle of Population,* 1st edition, 1798.

25. Paul Ehrlich, "Paying the Piper," *New Scientist* 36:652–55, reprinted in Garrett Hardin, ed., *Population, Evolution, and Birth Control,* 2nd ed. (San Francisco: W. H. Freeman, 1969), p. 127. See also Paul Ehrlich, *The Population Bomb* (New York: Ballantine, 1968), p. 36.

26. Food and Agriculture Organization of the United Nations, *World Agriculture: Towards 2015/2030,* Rome, 2002, p. 1, ftp://ftp.fao.org/docrep/fao/004/y3557e/y3557e01.pdf.

27. Editorial, "The World Food Crisis," *The New York Times,* April 10, 2008.

28. Figures are from FAOSTAT, statistics provided by the UN Food and Agriculture Organization, http://faostat.fao.org.

29. Food and Agriculture Organization, *Crop Prospects and Food Situation,* No. 2, April 2008. Available at www.fao.org/docrep/010/ai465e/ai465e04.htm.

30. Erik Marcus, *Meat Market: Animals, Ethics, and Money* (Ithaca, N.Y.: Brio Press, 2005), pp. 255–56, citing W. O. Herring and J. K. Bertrand, "Multi-trait Prediction of Feed Conversion in Feedlot Cattle," Proceedings of the 34th Annual Beef Improvement Federation Annual Meeting, Omaha, Nebraska, July 10–13, 2002, www.bifconference.com/bif2002/BIFsymposium_pdfs/Herring_02BIF.pdf, and "Pork Facts, 2001/2002," National Pork Board, Des Moines, Iowa.

31. Population Reference Bureau, 2007 World Population Data Sheet, pp. 1, 7, www.prb.org/pdf07/07WPDS_Eng.pdf.

32. Garrett Hardin, "Living on a Lifeboat," *Bioscience* 24 (1974), pp. 561–68.

33. Population Reference Bureau, 2007 World Population Data Sheet, p. 4, www.prb.org/pdf07/07WPDS_Eng.pdf.

34. See Amartya Sen, "Population: Delusion and Reality," *The New York Review of Books* 41:15 (September 22, 1994). An updated (2002) version is available at www.asian-affairs.com/issue17/sen.html.

35. See www.psi.org/reproductive-health and www.ippf.org/en.

36. Kwame Anthony Appiah, *Experiments in Ethics* (Cambridge, MA.: Harvard University Press, 2008), p. 198.

8. *Your Child and the Children of Others*

1. Quotes from Kravinsky come from Ian Parker, "The Gift," *The New Yorker,* August 2, 2004, from my own conversations with Kravinsky, and from his remarks to my classes.

2. Contrast S. A. Azar et al., "Is Living Kidney Donation Really Safe?" *Transplantation Proceedings* 39 (2007), pp. 822–23, with I. Fehrman-Ekholm et al., "Kidney Donors Live Longer," *Transplantation* 64 (1997), pp. 976–78, and E. M. Johnson et al., "Complications and Risks of Living Donor Nephrectomy," *Transplantation* 64 (1997), pp. 1124–28. For survival rates, see MayoClinic.com, "When Your Kidneys Fail," www.mayoclinic.com/health/kidney-transplant/DA00094.

3. For information on Paul Farmer, I am indebted to Tracy Kidder's fine biography, *Mountains Beyond Mountains* (New York: Random House, 2003), and Tracy Kidder, "The Good Doctor," *The New Yorker,* July 10, 2000.

4. Ian Parker, "The Gift," *The New Yorker,* August 2, 2004.

5. Genesis 22.

6. Ian Parker, "The Gift," *The New Yorker,* August 2, 2004.

7. Bruno Bettelheim, *Children of the Dream* (London: Macmillan, 1969); Melford Spiro, *Children of the Kibbutz* (New York: Schocken, 1975); N. A. Fox, "Attachment of Kibbutz Infants to

Mother and Metapelet," *Child Development* 48 (1977), pp. 1228–39.

9. Asking Too Much?

1. Liam Murphy, *Moral Demands in Nonideal Theory* (New York: Oxford University Press, 2000), p. 76. Murphy notes that a similar view has been outlined by Derek Parfit, *Reasons and Persons* (Oxford, UK: Clarendon Press, 1984), pp. 30–31 (although Parfit does not support it), and also by L. J. Cohen, "Who Is Starving Whom?" *Theoria* 47 (1981), pp. 65–81 and several others. For details, see Murphy, *Moral Demands,* p. 136, n. 8. See also Kwame Anthony Appiah, *Cosmopolitanism* (New York: Norton, 2006), pp. 164–65.

2. Kwame Anthony Appiah, *Cosmopolitanism* (New York: Norton, 2006), pp. 164–65.

3. Susan Foster et al., "Alcohol Consumption and Expenditures for Underage Drinking and Adult Excessive Drinking," *Journal of the American Medical Association* 289 (2003), pp. 989–95.

4. Jeffrey Sachs, *The End of Poverty* (New York: Penguin Press, 2005), chapter 15. Both the $124 billion and the $20 trillion are expressed in 1993 U.S. dollars, purchasing power adjusted. In 2008 dollars, the figures would be roughly 50 percent higher.

5. See UN Millennium Project, *Investing in Development: A Practical Plan to Achieve the Millennium Development Goals* (New York: Earthscan, 2005), chapter 17, www.unmillenniumproject .org/reports. The figures are in 2003 dollars.

6. Branko Milanovic, *Worlds Apart: Measuring International and Global Inequality* (Princeton, N.J.: Princeton University Press, 2005), p. 132.

7. For further arguments against the fair-share view, see Elizabeth Ashford, "The Demandingness of Scanlon's Contractualism," *Ethics* 113 (January 2003), pp. 273–302, and Garrett Cullity, *The Moral Demands of Affluence* (Oxford, UK: Oxford University Press, 2004), pp. 357–83.

8. Liam Murphy, *Moral Demands in Nonideal Theory* (New York: Oxford University Press, 2003), p.133.

9. Richard Miller, "Beneficence, Duty and Distance," *Philosophy and Public Affairs* 32 (2004), pp. 357–83.

10. Garrett Cullity, *The Moral Demands of Affluence* (Oxford, UK: Oxford University Press, 2004). There is much more in Cullity's book than I have discussed here. I have responded to some of the other arguments in my review in *Philosophy and Phenomenological Research* 75:2 (September 2007), pp. 475–83.

11. Brad Hooker, *Ideal Code, Real World: A Rule-Consequentialist Theory of Morality* (Oxford, UK: Clarendon Press, 2000), p. 166.

10. A Realistic Approach

1. Immanuel Kant, *Groundwork of the Metaphysics of Morals,* part II; for a more explicit discussion, see Kant's *Perpetual Peace,* appendix II.

2. John Rawls, *A Theory of Justice,* rev. ed. (Cambridge, MA.: Harvard University Press, 1999), p. 112.

3. See Richard Arneson, "What Do We Owe to Distant Needy Strangers?" in Jeffrey Schaler (ed.), *Peter Singer Under Fire* (Chicago: Open Court, forthcoming 2009).

4. For Gates's speech, see www.gatesfoundation.org/MediaCenter/ Speeches/Co-ChairSpeeches/BillgSpeeches/BGSpeech WHA-050516.htm?version=print; see paragraph 7 and concluding paragraph.

5. The estimate comes from the real estate site www.zillow.com, accessed October 12, 2008. See www.zillow.com/HomeDetails .htm?o=North&zprop=49118839.

6. *Forbes,* September 20, 2007.

7. Laura Rich, *The Accidental Zillionaire* (New York: Wiley, 2003), p. 175.

8. "Paul Allen's Yachts," www.yachtcrew-cv.com/paulallen.htm.

9. "The World's Billionares: #14, Lawrence Ellison," *Forbes,* March 5, 2008, www.forbes.com/lists/2008/10/billionaires08 _Lawrence-Ellison_JKEX.html.

10. Calculated on the Jetta getting 88,000 miles on that quantity of diesel, and the average American driver doing 12,000 miles a year.

11. Jennifer Lee, "He Made His Money on a Whim, but Now He's Got a Serious Idea," *The New York Times,* November 14, 2005; see also http://10over100.org.

12. The figures that follow draw on work by Thomas Piketty and Emmanuel Saez, based on U.S. tax data for 2006. Their figures are for pretax income, and include income from capital gains. For simplicity, I have rounded the figures. Note, too, that the numbers refer to "tax units," that is, in many cases, to families rather than to individuals. The figures can be found on Emmanuel Saez's website, http://elsa.berkeley.edu/~saez/.

13. Bill Clinton, *Giving* (New York: Knopf, 2007), p. 206.

14. Arthur Brooks, "The Poor Give More," www.CondéNast Portfolio.com, March 2008, citing the 2000 Social Capital Community Benchmark Survey, www.portfolio.com/news-markets/national-news/portfolio/2008/02/19/Poor-Give-More-to-Charity.

15. Ibid.

16. "Rich" is defined here in accordance with the definition given by Branko Milanovic and mentioned in the previous chapter. The figures are also from Milanovic, *Worlds Apart: Measuring International and Global Inequality* (Princeton, N.J.: Princeton University Press, 2005), p. 132.

17. According to OECD purchasing power parity figures, in 2006 the U.S. GDP was 36 percent of the OECD total. See http://lysander.sourceoecd.org/vl=3923031/cl=14/nw=1/rpsv/figures_2007/en/page4.htm.

18. Allowing for inflation since the report of the UN task force in 2007 would bring the figures down to seven times the estimated total amount required, and eighteen times the shortfall.

19. Buddha, *Dhammapada,* sec. 9, stanza 118, in T. Byrom, ed., *Dhammapada: The Sayings of the Buddha* (Boston: Shambhala, 1993), cited by Jonathan Haidt, *The Happiness Hypothesis* (New York: Basic Books, 2006), chapter 8. Plato, *The Republic,* 354.

20. *The Philosophy of Epicurus,* G. K. Strodach, trans. (Chicago: Northwestern University Press, 1963), p. 297. Cited by Haidt.

21. Arthur Books, "Why Giving Makes You Happy," *New York Sun,* December 28, 2007. The first study is from the Social Capital Community Benchmark Survey, while the second is from the University of Michigan's Panel Study of Income Dynamics.

22. J. A. Piliavin, "Doing Well by Doing Good: Benefits for the Benefactor," in C.L.M. Keyes and J. Haidt (eds.), *Flourishing: Positive Psychology and the Life Well-Lived* (Washington, D.C.: American Psychological Association, 2003), pp. 227–47; S. L. Brown, R. M. Nesse, A. D. Vinokur, and D. M. Smith, "Providing Social Support May Be More Beneficial Than Receiving It: Results from a Prospective Study of Mortality," *Psychological Science* 14 (2003), pp. 320–27; P. A. Thoits and L. N. Hewitt, "Volunteer Work and Well-being," *Journal of Health and Social Behavior* 42 (2001), pp. 115–31. I owe these references to Jonathan Haidt, *The Happiness Hypothesis* (New York: Basic Books, 2006), chapter 8.

23. William T. Harbaugh, Ulrich Mayr, and Daniel Burghart, "Neural Responses to Taxation and Voluntary Giving Reveal Motives for Charitable Donations," *Science,* vol. 316, no. 5831 (June 15, 2007), pp. 1622–25.

24. For more information about Henry Spira, see Peter Singer, *Ethics into Action: Henry Spira and the Animal Rights Movement* (Lanham, MD.: Rowman and Littlefield, 1998).

Index

PETER SINGER was born in Melbourne, Australia, in 1946, and educated at the University of Melbourne and the University of Oxford. He has taught at the University of Oxford, La Trobe University, and Monash University, and has held several other visiting appointments. Since 1999 he has been Ira W. DeCamp Professor of Bioethics at the University Center for Human Values at Princeton University, and since 2005, Laureate Professor at the University of Melbourne, attached to the Centre for Applied Philosophy and Public Ethics.

Peter Singer first became well known internationally after the publication of *Animal Liberation*. He is the author of many other books, as well as of the major entry on ethics in the current edition of the *Encyclopaedia Britannica*. Two collections of his writings have been published: *Writings on an Ethical Life*, which he edited, and *Unsanctifying Human Life*, edited by Helga Kuhse. He was the founding president of the International Association of Bioethics; a cofounder, with Paola Cavalieri, of The Great Ape Project; and is currently the president of Animal Rights International. In 2005, *Time* magazine named him "One of the 100 most influential people in the world."

Singer is married and has three daughters and three grandchildren. His recreations, apart from reading and writing, include hiking and surfing.

ABOUT THE TYPE

This book was set in Garamond, a typeface designed by the French printer Jean Jannon. It is styled after Garamond's original models. The face is dignified, and is light but without fragile lines. The italic is modeled after a font of Granjon, which was probably out in the middle of the sixteenth century.